WINTER BOOK

WINTER BOOK

HARRIET WEBSTER

Illustrated by
IRENE TRIVAS

ALADDIN BOOKS
Macmillan Publishing Company
New York

Aladdin Books
Macmillan Publishing Company
866 Third Avenue, New York, NY 10022
Collier Macmillan Canada, Inc.

First Aladdin Books edition 1988

Printed in United States of America

A hardcover edition of *Winter Book* is available from Charles Scribner's Sons, Macmillan Inc.

10   9   8   7   6   5   4   3   2   1

Library of Congress Cataloging-in-Publication Data

Webster, Harriet.
Winter book / Harriet Webster ; illustrated by Irene Trivas.—1st Aladdin Books ed.
p.   cm.
Summary: A collection of observations, information, projects, and activities related to
winter, from tracking animals and studying snowflakes to making Indian pudding.
Also includes a discussion of the season's holidays.
ISBN 0-689-71235-9 (pbk.)
1. Winter—Juvenile literature.   2. Holidays—Juvenile literature.
3. Amusements—Juvenile literature.   [1. Winter—Miscellanea.
2. Amusements.]   I. Trivas, Irene, ill.   II. Title.
QH81.W44 1988
793—dc19   88-1662   CIP   AC

For intrepid Ben, with great love.
May his spirit of discovery
forever endure and flourish.

Contents

WINTER BOOK

An Idea Book for Winter

The first snow of the season almost hypnotizes us, carries us into a dream, partly because of its beauty and partly, I think, because the first snow symbolizes what lies ahead. It reminds us that we are about to enter winter, when the world becomes a harsher place in which to live. Just as plants and animals are affected by the cold and dark, so too are we.

Winter Book is a collection of observations, information, projects, and activities related to winter. There are things to do indoors and out, alone or with company. There are projects to keep your hands busy and ideas to keep your mind churning. Simply put, the purpose of *Winter Book* is to help you make the most of the season that has the shortest days but seems to last the longest.

1
WARM AND SAFE

Dressing for the Cold

You've probably heard that normal body temperature is about 98.6°F. This temperature represents the balance between the heat your body produces and the heat it loses. Our very early ancestors relied on their own furry coats to keep them warm, but for thousands of years, as the course of evolution did away with that natural protection, human beings have relied on nature's resources to keep them warm. As early as 5000 B.C., cotton was cultivated in Mexico for use in clothing, and history shows that wool clothes were worn in Babylon (which means "the land of wool") by 4000 B.C.

The function of your clothing is not to provide heat but to serve as insulation. The warmth you feel when you go out into cold weather properly dressed is the heat generated by your own body. The clothing functions as a barrier that prevents heat from escaping.

Moisture, in the form of sweat, conducts heat away from the body, so in order to keep warm you need to keep dry. That's why it's important not to overdress. Runners who work out year-round often notice that they get cold when they wear too much clothing and sweat heavily. If sweat can't evaporate through your clothing, you'll feel cold.

Instead of one heavy layer of clothing, try wearing several lighter, looser layers. Air is trapped between the layers, providing extra insulation. Another way to fend off wind and wetness is to wear clothing with fibers that are tightly woven. The ideal winter fabric would also have lots of space between the fibers to trap air. And it would be "breathable," to allow moisture to evaporate from the body.

In truth, there is no such perfect fabric. Wool comes about the closest. Its natural curl makes it bulky, which means it can trap

extra air and serve as a good insulator. (Did you ever meet a sheep with straight hair?) And wool is naturally water-repellent. Wool yarn can be knit tightly, providing good protection against the wind. At the same time, wool can absorb about thirty percent of its own weight in moisture, which means it can absorb sweat and slowly let it evaporate instead of keeping it trapped against your skin.

When you dress to go out in the cold, think of the process as making a club sandwich. Build layers, perhaps starting with breathable thermal underwear. Add a T-shirt and then a wool sweater or a parka. If you plan to be active, be careful not to overdress since sweating will make you cold. Do be sure to wear a hat, since so much of the body's heat is lost through the head. If you're going ice-skating or if you tend to be bothered by freezing toes, try layering a pair of cotton socks or tights beneath wool socks to keep your feet extra warm.

Winter Health Hazards

We're all familiar with the common cold, and just about everyone comes down with a sore throat or a case of the sniffles sometime during the cold-weather months. But there are other winter health hazards.

Snow blindness is actually a sunburn of the corneal tissues of the eyes. Symptoms include redness, grittiness, headaches, and blurry vision. The eyelids sometimes swell, leading to temporary blindness. Symptoms may occur several hours after exposure to the sun. Snow blindness is best treated with cold compresses on the eyes and rest in a darkened room. If you are going to be out in the snow for a long time on a bright day, you might want to protect your eyes by wearing a pair of red- or brown-tinted sunglasses. Or make yourself a pair of snow goggles. (See page 7.)

You can get severe sunburn even in the coldest weather and on cloudy days, especially in snow-covered fields at high altitudes. The best way to avoid sunburn is to use a sun block or petroleum jelly.

Chilblains occur when the skin on hands or feet is repeatedly exposed to the cold and wet. It becomes severely dried and cracked. To avoid chilblains, dress properly and keep hands and feet dry and protected from the elements. Bag balm, a preparation used by farmers to soften the udders of milk cows in cold weather, can also be used by people to soften their cracked skin.

Hypothermia occurs when a person's body temperature drops below 98.6°F. The skin gets pale and the victim may experience uncontrollable shivers, dizziness, drowsiness, light-headedness, and nausea. The body feels stiff and painfully cold. The real danger occurs when the body temperature drops into the range of 82°–91°F. The best way to avoid hypothermia is to dress warmly and eat properly.

Frostbite usually occurs when a person is out in very cold weather, with strong winds, without wearing enough protective clothing. Ice crystals form *within* the skin cells and the skin becomes flushed, then white or grayish yellow. Fingers, toes, ears, nose, and heels are the most likely spots to be affected. The frostbitten area may hurt at first, but soon it will turn numb and cold.

To avoid frostbite, wear warm clothing, stay dry, and don't lace your footgear too tightly. To treat frostbite, cover the area with warm clothes and quickly get to a warm place. Drink hot liquids, and soak affected areas in warm water. Contrary to popular myth, it is never a good idea to rub a frostbitten area with snow since the skin can be permanently damaged by abrasion.

Chapped skin and lips are caused by exposure to dry air indoors and cold wind outside. In the process, the skin loses much of its natural moisture. Treat chapped hands, face, and lips by washing with warm water. Do *not* use soap on chapped skin. Treat with skin lotions and oils. Avoid licking your lips, and if your hands get really bad, coat them with petroleum jelly or hand lotion, and then protect them with a pair of cotton gloves. To avoid chapping, coat skin with petroleum jelly and wear protective lip cream.

Cabin fever, also called arctic hysteria, is a form of winter depression that exists among all people who live in northern areas. It is a sense of isolation and boredom that results from being shut in by bad weather. The best way to both avoid and treat cabin fever is to keep active. Pioneer farmers, pressed for time during the other seasons of the year, turned to crafts such as wood carving and toy making to alleviate their boredom. The Laps, Scandinavians, and North American Indians have all, at one time or another, showed their determination to stay alert and active in the cold by staging elaborate winter carnivals.

Making Snow Goggles

Usually a temporary problem, snow blindness occurs when the eyes are exposed to the sun's ultraviolet rays reflected off snow. Recovery is almost always complete and without complications.

Snow blindness, however, is easy to avoid. If you are going to be out in a bright sunny landscape all day—for example, while skiing—wear sunglasses. You can also fashion a pair of your own snow goggles. The Eskimos usually carved their goggles from bone or driftwood, making a narrow slit for each eye. Residents of other snowy areas, such as Siberia and Tibet, made their goggles from materials that included deer antlers, animal hides, bark, and braided horsehair. You can make a very simple pair out of cardboard.

The goggles will look like one of those basic eye masks sold at Halloween, except that the openings will be much narrower. After you cut out your mask, add ribbon or elastic ties to the sides so you can wear it. You might want to blacken the area around the eye slits to reduce glare. Do this by rubbing with a piece of charcoal or a black crayon. If birch bark is available, try making goggles out of that.

Keeping Cozy Indoors

Stitch pieces of old flannel nightgowns or pajamas into cozy patchwork bed sheets. All you have to do is cut the material into flat pieces (any size, any shape), iron them flat, and have an adult help you stitch them together with a sewing machine. Trim the edges until you have a rectangle eighty-four inches × sixty inches or larger (at least the size of your bed with an extra eighteen inches added on to both the length and the width for tucking in).

To avoid heat loss through your head, wear a nightcap!

In colonial times, our forefathers often heated bricks on the hearth, wrapped them in flannel, and stuck the bricks in the bottoms of their chilly beds to warm their feet. In the early 1800s, the fireplace was still the main source of heat in the home. If you wanted to sit and read somewhere away from the fireplace, you might have used a foot warmer.

A. Greely first patented such a device in 1813. He invented a metal box with a little door that closed securely. There was a handle on the box, so it could be carried from one part of the house to another. He shoveled embers from the fireplace into the box and clicked the door tightly closed. The embers stayed hot for several hours and the metal box prevented them from accidently starting a fire. Today, you can warm your feet comfortably and safely with a good reliable hot water bottle, or wear socks to bed.

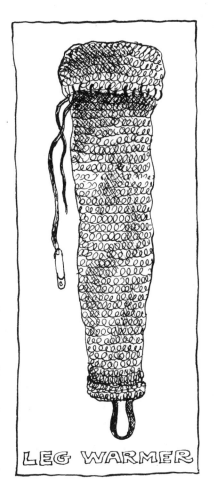

LEG WARMER

Make your own leg warmers. You'll need a worn-out adult-size sweater, needle and thread, and some elastic. Cut off the sleeves and cut to the length you want. (Measure your leg from ankle to knee and add one inch.) Turn inside out. Turn down top edge (where shoulder used to be attached) and sew in place to make a casing. Cut the elastic to fit snugly, then attach a safety pin to one end of the elastic to help guide it through the casing. Sew ends of elastic together. Add an elastic stirrup at the cuff to anchor the leg warmer to your foot. Turn right side out.

Add "warm" color accents—bright yellow, red, or orange—to your room. They might take the form of throw pillows, a bedspread, a cozy afghan, a poster, a picture you paint yourself. You could even dye a blanket canary yellow or tangerine. Avoid "cool" colors—blue, green, purple.

Make a draft dodger, also called a draft stopper, to prevent cold air from creeping in under windows and doors. Cut a piece of fabric about eight inches wide and four inches longer than the length of the windowsill or threshold in question. Fold it in half lengthwise, right sides together. Sew down the length and across one end. Then turn the tube right side out. Fill the tube with sand and stitch up the open end securely. Lay it across the window or doorway to block out icy drafts. For psychological warmth, make your draft dodger in a warm color or a bright print. (These make nice gifts.)

To turn your thoughts away from the bitter temperatures and wintry conditions brewing outside, try decorating your room with a few tropical plants purchased from a local nursery. They'll help turn your thoughts to warm weather and sun-drenched beaches. To give your plants a treat, put them in the bathroom when you take a steamy shower or bath. They'll feel as if they're back in the rain forest.

Bringing Nature Inside: Forcing Bulbs

There's nothing quite like a pot of fresh flowers to add cheer to a long winter's day. By planning ahead, you can have pots of tulips or paper-white narcissus blossoming in your house on the darkest, coldest winter days. You do it by "forcing" bulbs indoors.

Bulbs need a cycle of cool, cold, and then warm weather in order to produce flowers. During the cool and cold periods, which fall and winter provide, the bulb rests and then begins to develop a root system. When the weather gets warm, the bulbs begin to grow and eventually they blossom. To grow flowers indoors, you'll need to duplicate as much as possible the conditions nature provides out-

doors. Your object is to force bulbs to blossom when they normally would be sleeping.

The easiest way to force plants is to use the water-and-pebble method, which works particularly well with paper-white narcissus. Place two inches of pebbles in a flat pan that does not have a drainage hole. Place the bulbs flat side down into the pebbles, close but not touching each other or the sides of the pan. Pack more pebbles around the bulbs so that only the top half of each one is showing. Pour water into the pan until it reaches the bottom of the bulbs. Then put the pan in a dark, cool place for two to three weeks to give the roots a chance to develop.

Check daily, adding water when necessary to keep the bottoms of the bulbs wet. When there is a strong root system, take the pan out of the closet and place it in a sunny, warm spot. In a few weeks, you'll have a cluster of delicate fragrant white flowers, a preview of spring.

If you want to have fresh tulips growing in your house while it's cold and icy outdoors, begin by buying the largest bulbs you can find. Plant them in a short clay flowerpot. Put a few pebbles in the bottom of the pot to cover the drainage hole. Fill the pot half full with a regular potting-soil mixture, adding a little extra sand. Push the bulbs into the soil with the flat end down. Put them very close together, but not touching. Cover them with soil, leaving about ½ inch of the tops showing. Water the bulbs and then put the pot in an out-of-the-way corner of your refrigerator.

Leave it in there for ten weeks. That will give the bulbs enough time to develop their root systems. Then put the pot in a cool, dark place for another two weeks, until sprouts appear and grow to two inches. At this point, water the plants and bring them into the sunlight on a nice warm windowsill. Now you can treat them just as you would regular houseplants, watering them regularly so they don't dry out, turning the pot a little each day so the stalks don't bend over toward the sun. If the flowers become big and heavy, you may need to stake them to keep them from flopping over.

Making a Scatter Rug

Decorate your room with a handmade rug. First you'll need to build a wooden loom by nailing together straight two inch × two inch pieces of wood to form a rectangular frame slightly larger than the size of the rug you want to make. Using a ruler and pencil, mark off ½-inch intervals along two opposite sides of the loom. At each mark pound in a long nail, just far enough so the nail will stay firmly upright.

Take a long length of heavy cotton thread and wrap it around one nail. Draw it across to the opposite side, lengthwise, around a nail and back to the first side, continuing until you've worked your way all along the row of nails, from one end of the loom to the other. (Note: It's important that you use a single piece of thread for this process.)

Now you're ready to weave the weft. Cut strips of fabric about six inches wider than the width of the loom. (This is a good way to recycle old clothes. Just be sure to use all the same type of fabric,

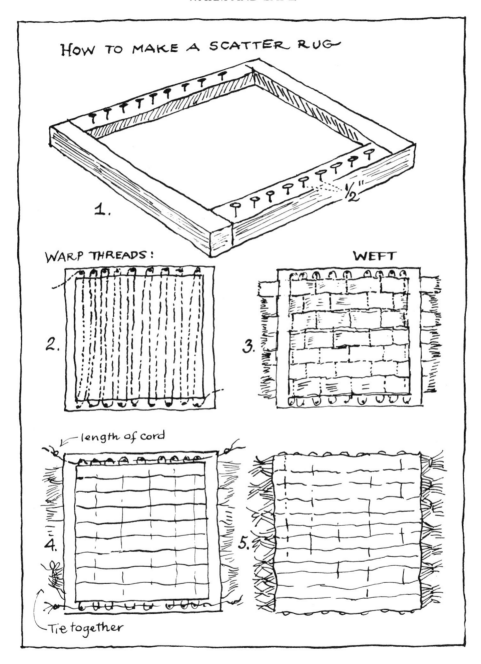

HOW TO MAKE A SCATTER RUG

1.

½"

WARP THREADS:

2.

WEFT

3.

length of cord

4.

Tie together

5.

so that all the material in the rug can be either dry-cleaned or washed.) Beginning at one corner, take one weft piece and weave it across the loom—over the first warp thread, under the second— all the way across. For the second row reverse the process—under the first warp thread, over the second. Keep alternating. Using your fingers, pull each piece snug up against the preceding one.

When you've filled in the entire frame, tie the warp threads with a length of cord so the woven strips won't slip loose. Then tie (use slipknots or half hitches if you know how) every two fabric-strip ends together. Use scissors to trim away extra fabric and to make fringe.

Cut the rug from the loom. Put it on your floor and enjoy.

Quilting

Early American pioneer women were very frugal. They hated to waste anything and took satisfaction in finding a new use for old things. When clothing wore out, they used the fabric to make patchwork quilts. To make them extra warm, they filled the quilts with pine needles, corn husks, or soft grasses. Without the time or materials for fancy stitchery, pioneer women often sewed their quilts together with twine or yarn.

To make your own quilt you will need a collection of fabric scraps. (If you use pieces of your own outgrown clothing, your quilt will be a personal history.) Be sure that all the scraps are washable.

You will also need a piece of cardboard, chalk, scissors, needle and thread, yarn scraps, darning needle, and a large piece of material for a backing (maybe an old cotton bedspread or sheet). If you want to make your quilt warm as well as pretty, you'll need an old blanket to use as the inside, in place of the pine needles and corn husks used by the pioneers. Here's how to make your quilt:

14

1. Cut a 6½-inch square from the cardboard. You will use this as a pattern. This size enables you to make six-inch squares, with enough material left over for a ¼-inch seam on each side.

2. Iron flat the pieces of fabric you are going to use.

3. Lay a piece of fabric on a hard flat surface (the floor, a table) and place the cardboard pattern on top. Trace the pattern with chalk, following the grain of the fabric. Cut out the square. Make another. Keep doing this until you have ninety-six squares, enough to make a four-foot × six-foot quilt.

4. When all the pieces are cut out, experiment by laying them on the floor in twelve rows of eight squares each. Try alternating dark and light squares, patterned ones and solid ones. When you get them just the way you want them, make a diagram, eight blocks across and twelve blocks long. Number each row.

5. Then group the squares together in bundles of eight, numbering each group to correspond with your diagram. Make a rough sketch to go with each group, showing how you plan to arrange the eight pieces to make a strip. (You can always change your mind later, but this way you'll have a record of the way you arranged them when you laid the whole quilt out.) Put a rubber band around each set and attach the sketch. You should have twelve sets.

6. To make a strip, take one set. Pin the front sides of two pieces together and sew across one edge with a "running stitch." Gather several stitches on a long, fine needle by weaving the point in and out of the fabric. Slide the stitches back onto the fabric without taking the needle out of the fabric. Repeat. Do this with the other pieces until all eight are attached. Now use an iron to press open the seams.

7. Follow this procedure until you have assembled all twelve strips. Once you've done this, you will use the same pinning, sewing, and pressing procedure to sew the strips together into a quilt top.

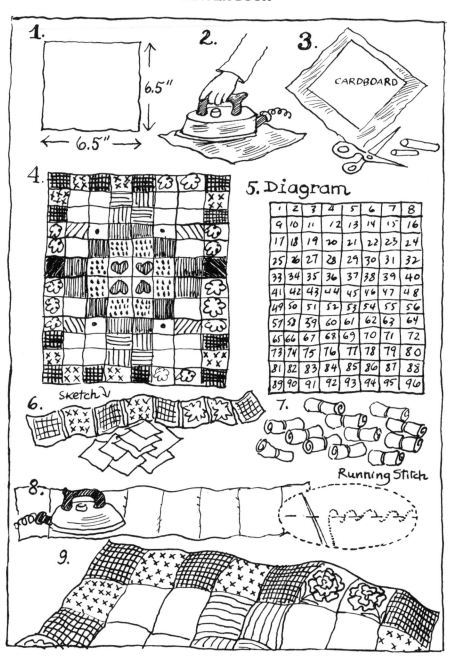

1.

6.5"

← 6.5" →

2.

3. CARDBOARD

4.

Sketch ↓

5. Diagram

1	2	3	4	5	6	7	8
9	10	11	12	13	14	15	16
17	18	19	20	21	22	23	24
25	26	27	28	29	30	31	32
33	34	35	36	37	38	39	40
41	42	43	44	45	46	47	48
49	50	51	52	53	54	55	56
57	58	59	60	61	62	63	64
65	66	67	68	69	70	71	72
73	74	75	76	77	78	79	80
81	82	83	84	85	86	87	88
89	90	91	92	93	94	95	96

6.

7.

Running Stitch

8.

9.

Keep in mind that making a patchwork quilt is a big project, especially if you are doing all the sewing by hand, as the early pioneers did. (If your family has a sewing machine and there's an adult who's willing to help you use it, the project will go much faster, of course.) When you finish making the quilt top, you will need to ask an adult to help you finish the quilt, following these steps:

1. Hem the quilt top around all four sides.
2. Cut sheet or blanket to be used for backing and hem all around so that it is the same size as the quilt top.
3. Cut filling (old blanket or commercial quilt batting) one inch narrower and one inch shorter than quilt top and backing.
4. Now make a sandwich. Place the backing on the floor, right side down. Add the filling, centering it carefully. Top off with the quilt top, right side up.
5. Have an adult help you pin the sandwich together. Use a running stitch to sew around the four sides.
6. Begin quilting, or tufting, by using a darning needle and brightly colored pieces of yarn to tie-off each corner and the center of each quilt block. Do this by putting the needle through the sandwich from the top of the quilt down through the backing and then pulling it up right next to where it went down. Tie the two yarn ends together with a knot. Trim ends to ½ inch or less. Repeat this process, making a knot at each corner of each block as well as in the center of each one. When you finish this process, your quilt is completed.

Don't worry if your stitches are uneven or your yarn knots aren't quite on the corners. No two patchwork quilts are ever the same—and that's why they're so special.

2
NATURE
IN WINTERTIME

Winter Weather

In the northern hemisphere, winter begins in December and is notable for its short days and cold weather, caused by the position of the earth on the path it follows as it revolves around the sun. In the southern hemisphere, winter begins in June.

The winter solstice in December marks the day the sun is at its lowest point on its journey across our sky. On this day, the shortest day of the year, the sun's rays fall directly over the farthest point south of the equator. Our winter concludes with the vernal equinox on March 21st, the day on which we experience equal hours of dark and light.

Our winter lasts one-fourth of the year; in the polar regions of the world, half the year is taken up by winter. Think about that the next time you're feeling tired of winter.

Using information from weather satellites high above the earth's surface, weather experts at the National Weather Service chart the movement and development of storms and storm systems. In addition to the photographs of the earth and the clouds provided by the satellites, the experts rely on radar. Radar signals indicate storm locations because they bounce off ice, hail, and raindrops high in the sky.

With up-to-the-moment information supplied by hundreds of weather stations across the country, the Weather Service Forecast Offices determine the direction and speed at which the weather is moving. These forecasts are then transmitted to airports, newspapers, and radio and television stations across the country so that people in each area know what to expect. Here are definitions of some of the terms you are likely to hear in a winter weather forecast:

Winter Storm Watch: This means there's a good chance that severe weather will move into your area. Keep tuned for further information.

Winter Storm Warning: The storm is about to strike. Take immediate steps to protect people and property.

Blizzard Warning: Heavy snow accompanied by winds of at least 35 m.p.h. can be expected shortly.

Severe Blizzard Warning: Heavy snow accompanied by winds of at least 45 m.p.h. and temperatures of 10°F. or lower can be expected shortly.

Ice Storm Warning: Rain is expected to freeze, leading to an accumulation of ice on streets, sidewalks, and fields.

Weather Folklore

Foretelling the weather was a popular pastime in rural America before the development of sophisticated weather-forecasting instruments and procedures. Farmers had to rely on their experience and intuition to help them "read" the weather. They passed their knowledge on from one generation to another, from one neighbor to another, gradually working their observations into sayings and proverbs that have become a part of our heritage. As a rule, the more local the sayings, the more reliable they tend to be.

Some weather beliefs can be scientifically proven and others are pure superstition. Still others fall into the "maybe" area. Many are delightfully fanciful. Let's take a look at some examples.

"Thunder in February frightens the maple syrup back into the ground." This New England saying may have some truth to it. Sap flows smoothly when there are freezing temperatures at night, with thawing temperatures during the day. A sudden warm spell, as would accompany a thunderstorm, could put a halt to the sap flow.

"Moonlit nights have the heaviest frost." This one is said to be true because frost does tend to form when the night is calm and the air cool. The moonlight shines brightest on such nights, so farmers were particularly alert for frost during a full moon.

"A green Christmas makes a fat churchyard." This shows the complex reasoning that lies behind some sayings. If the weather was mild and snowless (green) at Christmastime, folks would take off their toasty long underwear in order to wear fashionable clothes for the holidays. Consequently, many people would catch colds, develop pneumonia, and die.

"If corn husks are thicker than usual, a cold winter is ahead." Or,

"When the corn wears a heavy coat, so must you." Such sayings were popular in Pennsylvania but weather specialists don't set much store by them. The thick husk was caused by a warm, humid summer, and the belief was that such a summer would be followed by a particularly cold, dry winter.

Just as summer signs were considered predictors of the winter ahead, winter signs were considered indicators of the type of summer to expect, as shown in this saying:

> If February brings drifts of snow,
> There will be good summer crops to hoe.

Particularly popular in the south, this verse does have a scientific basis. A very cold and snowy winter can damage insect larvae as well as weed seeds, leading to fewer plant and animal pests the following spring. Combined with an ample quantity of water stored in the ground (accumulated from melting snowfall), this is an encouraging sign of a healthy growing season ahead.

"It's snowing for cats and ducks." A Pennsylvania German expression used to indicate that enough snow would fall to track a duck or cat through, this proverb shows how weather forecasting led to imaginative language. Here's another example: "When it snows,

the old woman is plucking her white geese." Still other proverbs are expressed in verse:

> Onion skins very thin,
> Mild winter coming in;
> Onion skins very tough,
> Winter's going to be very rough.

This saying originates in the Midwest and is thought to hold some truth.

Lots of sayings have developed around animal behavior. Weather experts say there's no truth to the belief that a hard winter lies ahead if the turkey feathers are especially thick by Thanksgiving. They can't seem to explain the thinking behind the belief that the amount of brown fur on the woolly bear foretells the severity of the oncoming winter, but opinion is divided as to whether there is any truth to this notion. On the other hand, crickets are generally accepted as good thermometers. They chirp faster in warm weather, slower in cold. According to folklorist Eric Sloane, if you count the chirps for fourteen seconds and then add forty, you'll have a pretty accurate idea of the temperature where the cricket is.

Another popular superstition holds that a hard winter is in the offing when the squirrels lay in a big store of nuts, but the truth is that squirrels stash away as many nuts as they can find and some years nuts are just easier to come by than other years.

Some animal weather sayings, like this one, originated with the Early American Indians:

> When you see a beaver
> Carrying sticks in its mouth,
> It will be a hard winter—
> You'd better go South.

The Indians believed that the beavers hustled to gather sturdy sticks in anticipation of a hard winter, that they sensed the need to fortify their lodges to protect them from the oncoming harsh weather. The saying is still popular in the Appalachian Mountain region, but scientists today do not consider such activity on the part of the beaver at all reliable in predicting the severity of the winter ahead.

Can you invent some weather proverbs of your own? Hint: Concentrate on the weather right in your own community, since that's the weather you know best.

Bird-Watching

The most important factor determining which birds can survive comfortably in the North during the winter and which ones must go south is the bird's ability to secure the necessary food in the face of cold and snow. Water plant life dies back in cold weather, strongly restricting food sources for water birds. Ponds and lakes freeze over, making it difficult or impossible for birds to get what little food there is. For this reason many water birds fly south or leave their inland territory and head for the open sea, where food is more accessible.

Insects in general cannot tolerate the cold, so they are usually dormant in the winter. This means that birds, such as flycatchers and warblers, that depend upon catching insects in the air, must fly south to find the airborne insects that make up their diet.

Snow also limits food sources for ground feeders, such as the robins and thrashers that feed on insects and small animals. The snow also shields the movement of mice and other small rodents, making it difficult for hawks and owls to stalk their prey.

Birds that can survive in the North through the cold months are those that feed on the hibernating insects and larvae and pupae that fill bark crevices and openings in tree trunks and limbs. About half the small winter birds, including woodpeckers, nuthatches, and chickadees, live off these. The other half, including finches, sparrows, and grosbeaks, depend on tree and weed seeds and shrub berries. Some winter birds take advantage of both these types of foods.

Birds have a high body temperature and those that stay North in the winter need to have sufficient food to metabolize in order to keep their bodies warm. A long period of snow cover can lead to scarcity in food supply, which in turn means that birds don't get enough to eat, their temperatures drop, and they freeze.

Even though many birds do migrate south, passing the winter in a warmer climate, winter is still a good season for bird-watching. Bare trees and bushes make it easier to locate the birds that do stay. Winter is also a good time to collect birds' nests because they're easier to spot and because the birds are no longer using them. If you look up at a bare tree and spot a nest with a roof of leaves, it's likely the birds have left and a wintering deermouse has moved in.

Snow on the ground also means that you can study bird tracks easily. Birds leave interesting tracks. Ground varieties such as the starling or pheasant show alternated tracks, one footprint in front of the other. Hopping and perching birds such as the sparrow or bluejay tend to leave paired tracks. Sprinkle birdseed around a muddy area or on packed snow to attract birds so you can become acquainted with their prints before taking a walk in the woods, along a beach, or wherever you plan to wander.

A bird's foot usually has four toes, three pointing frontward and one pointing backward. Some birds, such as goldfinches, juncos, and sparrows, move on the ground by hopping. They land on the snow with both feet, leaving paired tracks. Others, such as pigeons, crows, starlings, and pheasants, are walkers. They move by placing one foot in front of the other, leaving a row of single tracks. The track pattern then can be used to help identify the type of bird that made it.

To encourage birds to visit your yard, provide them with the food and water they need to sustain them through the cold weather when food supplies are scarce. Ideally they should have separate containers of water for drinking and bathing. Place the water in full sun to help keep it from freezing. Don't use metal containers because the birds' feet could freeze to them.

Most of the birds that are attracted to bird feeders are seedeaters. The best food to give seedeaters is packaged wild-bird seed mixture, cracked corn, sunflower seeds, and cereals. Some birds also favor ground-up dog biscuits and shelled nuts. Birds tend to form the habit of frequenting the same feeding spot, so if you decide to start feeding them, you should keep it up throughout the winter.

The simplest way to feed birds is to trample down the snow, scattering seeds on the surface. Do this only if you are sure there are no cats around. You can make a simple bird feeder for seedeaters by taking a piece of wood and nailing a simple rim around the outside to keep the seeds from blowing off. Drill holes in the board, run rope through the holes, and hang it from a tree.

The best foods for birds are seeds and suet, but in an emergency there are lots of good substitutes including bread crumbs, boiled potatoes, rice, crumbled eggs, apple cores, shredded lettuce or celery tops, and even small bits of meat. As we've shown, different birds have different food preferences. Insect-eating birds such as the titmouse, bluejay, and chickadee will eat suet. Sparrows, cardinals, and finches will be attracted by seeds. Robins and cedar waxwings like fruits and berries.

Many suet eaters favor peanut butter, but it's a good idea to mix it with cornmeal so the birds don't choke. Spread the mixture on sticks and place on the feeding surface. Other good choices for suet eaters include fat pork, sweet butter, cottage cheese, and lard mixed with cornmeal.

To make a simple feeder for suet eaters, you will need a small log and some rope for hanging. Drill one-inch holes several inches apart across the log. Fill the holes with peanut butter, suet, or one of the other foods mentioned above. Hang from a tree. Or fill half a grapefruit, lemon, lime, or orange skin with suet and hang from a tree or tuck into forked branches. Half a coconut shell makes a good feeder too, for either seeds or suet. Just drill two holes near the rim and hang. If you have some pinecones, you can roll them in a peanut butter-and-cornmeal mixture or in suet and hang them up. Old onion bags can also be filled with suet and tied to a tree.

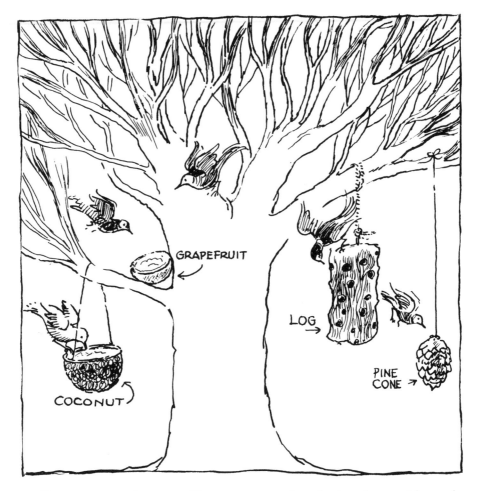

You can recycle your Christmas tree by placing it outside and "decorating" it regularly for the birds. Drape the tree with strings of unsalted popcorn, cranberries, grapes, raisins, and apple slices. Slip on stale doughnuts or dry pieces of bread. Add orange baskets and some of the other fruit-skin containers mentioned above. You can also make a bird tree by decorating a live tree in your yard.

Take a bird field guide out of the library to help you identify the birds that frequent your feeder. It's fun to keep a notebook chronicling your observations. Each time you see birds at your feeder, note the date, weather conditions, type of birds, eating habits, and any other behavior you may notice. You may also want to add sketches of the birds and of the tracks you find near the feeder after a snow.

Tracking Animals

At first glance, you may think that the entire animal kingdom has either gone into hibernation or migrated south for the winter. Sharpen your senses and take an early morning walk, however, and you will soon find much evidence of activity in the animal kingdom. One of the best ways to study animals at this time of year is to "collect" their tracks.

Animal tracks show up well after a snowfall. Begin your search soon after the sky clears, before other walkers smudge the prints and before the snow begins to melt. Winter tracks can be found in areas without snow as well. Check muddy spots by the banks of ponds and streams, where animals go to drink. Look also in sandy areas and along dirt pathways.

Different kinds of animals leave different kinds of tracks, and with practice you will be able to identify wildlife according to the prints left behind. Deer, moose, sheep, and goats leave hoofprints. Skunks and raccoons are almost flat-footed and their prints show nearly the entire footpad as well as the claws. Dogs and cats, like other members of the dog and cat families, make an imprint with their footpads and sometimes with their claws.

The hind prints of most animals appear to be in front of the forepaw prints and slightly to the outside of them. This is because the animals require the leverage supplied by strong rear legs for the next jump or step. This pattern is particularly evident in hopping animals like rabbits. Tree climbers place their front feet nearly next to each other when they jump while animals that move along the

Rabbit Tracks

Deer Tracks

Bird Tracks

Your Tracks

Squirrel Tracks

ground seldom leave paired forepaw prints; instead, one forepaw imprint is slightly ahead of the other. Both tree-climbing and ground animals, however, usually leave paired hind prints.

As you can see, the pattern of the prints as well as the size and shape can help you identify the animals that made the imprints. Tracks can also tell you if an animal was moving slowly or swiftly, or if he lay down to rest or eat. To become acquainted with track patterns, observe neighborhood cats and dogs in the snow. See how their prints differ when they run and when they walk.

The simplest technique for collecting prints is to sketch the tracks as accurately as possible. Take along a tape measure so you can measure the print at its longest and widest points, in order to make your sketch as true as possible. You can also photograph the prints. These methods can be used for prints made on any sort of surface, particularly a soft one such as snow.

If you track an animal in hardened mud, perhaps along a frozen dirt road or riverbank, you can bring the prints back home by making a casting. You will need a pair of scissors, plaster of Paris, water, stiff cardboard, and a pointed trowel. Press the cardboard into the ground around the print, using the trowel to make a depression if the ground is too hard to simply push in the cardboard. This frame or collar determines the size of your casting. Mix the plaster of Paris according to package directions, until it has the consistency of cake batter. Pour the mixture into the collar, completely filling it. Permit to harden (takes only a few minutes). Then, pull the collar and casting from the ground, using the trowel to pry loose if necessary. Remove the collar and clean off the face of the casting.

If there are prints in the snow right in your yard, you can make delicate castings by using melted paraffin. Paraffin is extremely flammable, however, so you must have an adult assisting you if you want to try this method. Begin by melting paraffin blocks or old candles in the top of a double boiler, with water in the bottom section. Pour over track sparingly. If you keep the layer of wax thin, it will freeze when it comes in contact with the snow without melting the track. Remove the hardened imprint from the snow.

Through sketches, photographs, and castings, you can record the imprints of the birds and animals that live in your neighborhood, even in wintertime. Be sure to label each addition to your collection with a tag noting the date and location where the print was found and the probable identity of the animal it belonged to. You will be surprised at the variety of imprints you accumulate.

3
WINTER FUN

Studying Snowflakes

Johannes Kepler (1571–1630), a German mathematician and astronomer, was the first scientist to recognize that all snowflakes have six sides. Wilbur Bentley (1865–1931) of Vermont was one of the first people to photograph snowflakes. He caught them on glass slides and photographed them under his microscope. His pictures are called photomicrographs. Bentley was so involved in recording the endless variety of six-sided forms that he became known as Snowflake Bentley.

To study snowflakes yourself, begin by collecting samples of falling snow on a dark cloth or a piece of black construction paper. Examine the snowflakes with a magnifying glass and make sketches of what you see. While each one has six sides or points, no two are exactly the same. The three most common types are stellar (a starlike flake with six projecting ice crystals), plate (six-sided flat flakes), and hexagonal plate (with crystal extensions).

Contrary to popular belief, snowflakes are not frozen raindrops. Sleet, hail, and icicles are made from frozen water but snow develops from water vapor, a layer of water in the upper air so fine that it is invisible. When the water vapor freezes, it turns into tiny ice crystals,

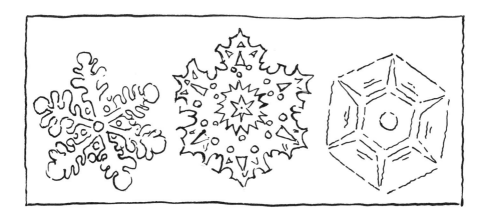

or snowflakes. Droplets of water within a cloud can also become ice crystals or snowflakes. Often the snowflakes grow as they travel toward earth through the moist air, collecting dust particles. Sometimes they hit a warm layer, melt, and fall as raindrops.

Each snowflake is composed of thousands of ice crystals. Molecules of water vapor in the cold winter clouds are attracted to dust particles, frozen cloud droplets, and small particles of ice. These particles become the nuclei or center of the snowflake, and it is to the nuclei that the molecules attach themselves in an ice-crystal pattern. The particles continue to grow until their weight makes them begin falling to earth.

All clouds, however, are not the same. Just as some clouds are colder than others and some contain more moisture than others, different clouds produce different flake patterns. Warm, moist clouds usually produce big, feathery, snowflakes that resemble stars. Cold, moderately moist clouds tend to produce plate flakes.

If you would like to watch ice crystals form, leave a pane of glass outside overnight. The next morning, when the temperature is still below freezing, pour some hot water on it and watch what happens.

To examine snowflakes in more detail, you'll need a microscope, slides, and a spray can of clear lacquer or clear plastic. Store your slides and lacquer or plastic in the freezer until it snows and you are ready to undertake the project. Then take them outside. Work quickly so they don't have time to warm up. Put a slide on a piece of wood so the heat from your hand doesn't warm it. Spray the slide with a thin coat of lacquer or plastic. Hold the board out in the snow until several flakes have fallen onto the slide. Then place the slide on a second board, out-of-doors but out of the snowfall (perhaps under a table). Make several slides this way. Let them dry outside for an hour, then bring them indoors to examine under a microscope. See if you can identify the different types of snowflakes.

Want to make your own permanent snowflakes? Cut a circle of paper six inches or more in diameter. Fold it in half. Then fold it in thirds. Fold in half once more. Cut notches and shapes along the edges to make a design. Unfold your snowflake.

Snow Experiments

It would take about sixteen to thirty-two snowflakes in a row to cover one inch. Some snowflakes are much smaller, while others grow to half an inch. Fluffy and irregular, snowflakes form air pockets between one another as they pile up. If you collect ten inches of snow in a container and let it melt, you'll end up with only about one inch of water. That's because snow is about one part ice crystals to ten parts air. The high proportion of air is also part of the reason that snowflakes sparkle. As the flakes take shape, tiny reflecting surfaces form in the air spaces between the ice crystals and the sun bounces off these surfaces.

You can do additional experiments by melting samples of wet snow and then of dry snow, always using the same size sample (ten inches in depth) so you can make accurate comparisons. How much more water is there in the wet snow? To learn how the age of the snow affects its water content, melt a fresh sample, a day-old sample, and an even older sample.

Another interesting fact about snow is that even though the flakes appear light and delicate as they plummet from the sky, snow can become very heavy. Ten inches of snow on the roof of an average 1,500-square-foot building weighs about forty tons. You can weigh a bucket of snow on your bathroom scale, but be sure to weigh the empty container first so you can subtract its weight from the total.

Snow acts as an insulator, protecting plants from the wind, ice, and cold. Like a huge blanket, it helps warm mice, worms, moles, chipmunks, and other animals that winter beneath the ground. To see for yourself how well snow insulates, try a simple experiment. You'll need two thermometers. Bury one in snow and hang the other one from a branch in the shade. Check after an hour to see which shows a colder reading. Is it colder in the air or beneath the snow? If you decide to dig a snow cave, take the temperature outside the cave and within, always leaving the thermometer in place for an hour. Which is warmer?

It's easy to find out which parts of your yard are the warmest and which are the coldest. Just make a group of snowballs the same size. Put one in an elevated place, one on the doorstep, one on a patch of bare ground, another on the sidewalk. Try to guess the order in which the snowballs will melt and then compare your conclusions with what actually happens.

Snow can be both helpful and harmful. It can improve the quality of the soil, leaving it moist and loose when the snow melts away in the spring. Too much snow, however, can prevent animals from reaching their food and can damage trees by breaking branches with its weight. A deep snow combined with a fast spring melt can bring serious flooding conditions. And, of course, snow brings all sorts of recreational opportunities but it also makes for hazardous driving conditions.

Salt is the main ingredient used in removing snow and ice from slippery roads. Salt dissolves in water and eventually seeps into the soil, killing grass and other plants. To see for yourself how harmful salt can be to plant life, you'll need two small plants of the same kind. Keep them in the same place. Water them regularly with the same amount of water, but give one plain water and the other water to which you've added a teaspoon of salt (the kind used for salting roads and sidewalks, if possible). Observe the results.

If you want to keep track of the amount of snow that falls in your neighborhood during each storm, make a snow gauge. You'll need a large can or a widemouthed jar and some masking tape. (If you live in an area where it snows a great deal, you'll need a taller container, perhaps a metal wastebasket.) Use a ruler to mark inches on the tape, making your first mark one inch from the bottom of the strip. Attach the tape to the inside of the container, with the one-inch marking one inch from the bottom. Place the container in an open area away from the house and from trees. Check the gauge each day snow falls. Make a chart recording the date, the amount of snow that fell, and the total amount so far this winter. Be sure to empty the can each time you take a reading so you can begin again. At the end of the season, compare your records with the total amount of snowfall reported by the local weather service.

If there has been a lot of snow in your area this winter, you can study a snowbank. With a shovel, take a top-to-bottom slice out of the bank. You'll probably find several dark layers inside. Each one marks the end of a snowfall and is formed by the dirt particles that settle on the top of a snowfall. Count the layers for an estimate of how many times it snowed.

Making a Snow Sculpture

Tired of making snowmen? Eager for a new challenge? Then try a snow sculpture. Here's a project that requires few materials but lots of imagination and energy. Any number of friends can be part of the fun. Just be certain to plan your project according to the number of helpers on hand.

Timing is crucial. First, choose a day with subfreezing temperatures and plenty of snow on the ground. Second, it is important that several additional days of subfreezing conditions are anticipated.

Before digging into the snow, do some planning. Decide what

shape you want to sculpt. Try to choose a subject without too much detail. (Sculpting a recognizable person is very difficult.) Then rule a piece of blank paper into one-inch squares. Letting one inch on paper equal one foot, make a drawing of your sculpture on this grid. As a general rule, a four-person team working very hard can complete in one day the snow mound needed for a six-foot high by six-foot wide snow sculpture.

Begin your outdoor work by making a large mound of snow, using old boards to support the sides. Soak the mound with water and then stomp on it. Shovel on more snow, soak, and stomp again. Repeat this process until you have a block of packed snow at least a foot taller and wider than your planned sculpture. For large projects, this step can take more than one day.

Once you have completed the mound, use your hands to mold the snow into a rough approximation of your proposed sculpture. Let the rough form stand overnight. The next morning, when it is frozen solid, use chisels to carve the details.

When you have completed the form to your satisfaction, spray your sculpture with a light stream of water. Be certain the temperature is at least five degrees below freezing before beginning this step. Use a plastic spray-pump bottle or a garden hose hooked up to an indoor tap and routed out the window. (Outdoor faucets have probably been turned off for the winter.) Once sprayed, the sculpture will take on a glossy appearance.

Students at Dartmouth College in Hanover, New Hampshire, have been sculpting snow since 1927. Some of the better-known creations included in their annual Winter Carnival have been a St. Bernard dog twenty feet high, a King Kong statue tall enough to peer into a second-story window, and a huge Mickey Mouse. A project like one of these requires about 80 people, 250 tons of snow, and 500 working hours to complete.

Making Your Own Sled

If you like woodworking projects, you might like to make your own sled. You'll need a pair of old wooden skis, a sheet of plywood ⅜ inch thick cut to the size you want your sled to be, a four-foot-long piece of lumber measuring two inches thick by two inches wide (this is called a two-by-two), wood screws, sandpaper, and either varnish, paint, or polyurethane.

1. Drill a hole into the front of the plywood body so that you will be able to attach a rope to the completed sled.
2. Cut the two-by-two into four pieces of equal length. Sand the pieces smooth.
3. Sand the plywood body of the sled.
4. Brush the pieces of two-by-two and the body with a coat of varnish, paint, or polyurethane. Allow to dry thoroughly.
5. Remove bindings from skis. Sand and finish as in Step 4, if needed.
6. From the underside of each ski, use wood screws to attach two pieces of two-by-two to top of each ski. Leave screw heads flush or countersunk.
7. Use wood screws to attach body to top of two-by-twos, bridging the two skis.
8. Add pull rope and you're ready to go.

Having Fun in the Snow

You can make a snow shield out of a large piece of heavy cardboard. Cut it into two circles the size you want your shield to be; tape the two together. Thread duct tape or multiple thicknesses of masking tape through the center of the shield and back again, to form a loop for your arm to go through. Make another loop at the edge of

the shield as a handgrip (use lots of tape to make this one as rigid as possible). If you need a shield in a hurry, try using a garbage-can lid.

Make fruit slush by pouring fruit juice over a glass of fresh snow. You can make simple ice cream by mixing fresh-fallen snow with sugar or honey. For each serving, use one cup of snow and a teaspoon of sweetener.

Use packed snow or chalk to make a snowball target by outlining a series of concentric circles (a small one surrounded by a larger one, which is surrounded by a still larger one, and so on) on a smooth outdoor wall. Decide how many points to give each ring. Have each contestant make a pile of ten snowballs and see who gets the highest score.

To make your own snowplow, all you'll need is a hammer and nails, several feet of rope, and several old boards. The drawing on the facing page shows how to assemble the plow. Weight your plow down with a friend and use it to clear paths or to pack down snow for a slide. To make a good slide, pour or spray water over a two-foot-wide track of packed snow on level or slightly slanted ground. Travel down the track on a piece of cardboard or linoleum or on a plastic garbage bag.

Snow angels are quick, easy, and fun to make. Lie down in fresh snow, flat on your back with your arms outstretched. Make wings by moving your arms gently up and down. Get up carefully and step away from your angel. You can make a whole scene of angels, sometimes moving your head and legs as well as your arms.

Design a full-size house floor plan in the snow, marking out the walls by tramping through the snow.

Inner tubes and old cafeteria trays are great makeshift sleds. So are flattened-out cardboard boxes. Want to slide with friends? A large appliance box can carry several riders.

If you have lots of outdoor play space—woods and fields, a big park—you can play trail makers. Give one player ten minutes to set a trail in the snow that will challenge his followers. He might include dead ends and circles that join with other circles. To further confuse the picture, he might walk along a fence or stone wall, or even interrupt the trail by climbing a tree and swinging to a second tree. The more inventive he is, the more fun the game.

You can find signs of spring in the late winter by scraping away the snow at the base of trees. Look for fresh moss and young ferns. They usually appear first on the east and south sides of the tree.

Snow Artistry

Lay an old, empty picture frame on the ground. Pack the opening tightly with snow. Spray snow with light mist of water and let freeze overnight. Mix powdered poster paints to pastelike consistency and paint a picture on the ice. Then bring the whole frame and picture into the house. Place it on a thick bed of newspaper and let colors thaw slightly. Take the picture outside and refreeze. You can use your snow painting in a snow-sculpture scene or set it into the side of a snowhouse.

For a stained-glass effect, try making a painting on an old storm window or a pane of glass. Outline a design by dividing the glass into sections with low walls of plasticene. Then use food coloring to color several containers of water. Pour colored water into each of the sections and allow to freeze overnight. Insert the window in a snowhouse or snow sculpture and illuminate by placing a flashlight behind it.

For more active artistry, brighten several bowls of water with food coloring. Gather together your collection of water pistols and fill each one with a different color water. Then "shoot" pictures in the snow.

On a frosty night, welcome guests with snowlights placed by your front door. Color well-packed snowballs by dipping them quickly into cold colored water. For snowballs too large to dip, put colored water in a spray bottle and mist them lightly. Place snowballs around large flashlights.

Frost and Frost Prints

Frost is formed when the air at the surface of the ground cools and loses some of its moisture. The moisture is deposited on the ground in the form of dew. On a clear, still, subfreezing night hoarfrost forms instead of dew, coating the grass and ground with a blanket of frost.

Frost forms on the windowpanes when the air outside is cold enough to chill the air inside, wherever the indoor air touches the window glass. (Frost seldom forms where storm windows are in use because they prevent outside air from chilling the inside air.)

To study frost, take a walk outdoors very early some freezing cold morning. Observe the way the ice coats individual blades of grass, dirt, and plants. Indoors, use a magnifying glass to examine frost on the windows. To form a new design, blow on a small patch of the glass. The warmth of your breath will melt the frost. Soon it will re-form into a new pattern.

To make a frost print, you'll need some blueprint paper (from an art-supply store), tape, and peroxide. The procedure works best on a bright, sunny, freezing cold day. Press the sensitive side of the blueprint paper to the frosty glass and anchor with tape. Within a few minutes, the sunlight will turn the paper light blue, and the frost design will be imprinted in white.

To preserve the design, immerse the paper in water for a couple of minutes. Then immerse it in water containing a tablespoon of peroxide. Let the print dry flat. You might want to make a collage from a series of frost prints.

Your Own Winter Carnival

Break the tedium of a long winter by staging a lively winter carnival, just as they've done for over a hundred years in St. Paul, Minnesota. The St. Paul Carnival is a week-long event, ruled by King Boreas, the ruler of the North Wind, and the Queen of Snows. Boreas is overthrown by his enemy, Vulcan, King of Fire, ushering in the approach of spring. This scene is performed in front of ten thousand people. The festival also features competitions in ski jumping, speed skating, ice hockey, dogsledding, tobogganing, curling, ice fishing, and ice carving.

Invite a group of friends to help you plan your carnival. You might decide to invent and stage your own skit about the end of winter and the arrival of spring. Set your imagination loose! Then decide what kinds of contests you want to have. Sack races in the snow? A snow obstacle course? A snowball-throwing contest? A scavenger hunt? Gather all the equipment you'll need. Next, plan and prepare a winter picnic of hot drinks and high-calorie foods to keep you warm outdoors.

Invite some parents to join the celebration. You might all decide to build an enormous snowman or snowwoman together. Be sure to appoint one person the official carnival photographer to document all the fun on film.

Safety on Ice

Just as you should never go swimming alone, you should never play or skate on ice without a companion. Safe skating requires that you combine common sense and caution with knowledge of ice conditions. Before crossing a frozen span of water, be certain it is strong enough to bear your weight.

"Black" ice is the only really safe ice. (The colder and harder ice gets, the clearer it becomes and the darker it looks as you stare at the pond beneath.) Salt-water ice is usually unsafe. A rule of thumb: any ice less than three inches thick is not safe. Ice four to five inches thick is considered strong enough to support a group of skaters; but even then, there may be exceptions. A sudden thaw can weaken even very thick ice to the danger point. Near the end of winter, old ice as thick as eight inches may be unsafe due to "honeycombing," a pattern of air pockets created by frequent thawing and freezing. Remember too that even when ice is solid and safe in the center of the pond, the edges can be dangerously thin.

If you or a companion should fall through the ice, follow the rescue procedures outlined below. Remember that it only makes the situation worse to have the rescuer also fall through, so don't take any unnecessary risks. In all rescue procedures, distribute your weight and that of any assistants over as large an area of ice as possible.

Saving Yourself

1. If it is necessary to cross unfamiliar ice, carry a pole that is ten feet to twelve feet long. If you fall through the ice, you can suspend the pole across the opening in the ice and use it for support in climbing out of the hole.

2. If you cross ice on skis or snowshoes, loosen bindings first so you can slip them off should you fall through.

3. If you fall through, spread arms wide out to the sides and flutter kick to keep from floating under the ice. Break through thin ice and head for thicker ice.

4. Lunge forward on to thicker ice with a sturdy kick; when your hips are up on the ice, raise hands over head and roll away from the hole. Continue to roll until you are a safe distance away.

5. Roll in snow to absorb water from your clothes. Get warm and dry as soon as possible.

Saving Someone Else

1. If the pond is equipped with a life buoy and long rope, throw the buoy to the victim. Otherwise, extend a pole, ladder, branch, or plank to the victim, lying on your stomach to distribute your weight. Slowly draw the victim to the edge of the hole. (If nothing else is available, hold out your scarf, belt, sweater, or jacket.)

2. If there are other skaters nearby, you can form a human chain. Each person lies on his stomach and grips the ankles of the person in front. The person at the head of the chain either extends a branch or other object to the victim or grabs his wrists and draws him gently from the water as the entire chain wriggles slowly backward.

Ice Shuffleboard

Ice shuffleboard takes advance preparation. You'll need to ask an adult to help you use a jigsaw to cut out twelve plywood discs, each five inches in diameter. Paint half the discs one color and half another. Make cues out of a lightweight wood, like pine. The cues should be about 4 inches wide, 1 ¼ inches thick, and 8 feet long. Place one of your discs across the bottom of the cue. Use a pencil to trace the curve of the disc on the cue. Then use the jigsaw to cut along the pencil line, matching the bottom of the cue to the curve of the disc. Use sandpaper to smooth away splinters.

At the skating pond, mark a series of concentric circles in the smooth ice to form a target. Decide how many points each circle

is worth. Mark a starting line about twelve feet from the target. To play, skate to the line pushing a disc in front of your cue, giving it a push before your skate crosses the starting line.

The idea is to see who can score the most points on the target. Before you start to play, decide how many points make a game. Alternate shots with your opponent, knocking each other's discs off the target. After you have each shot all four of your discs, add up the points of the discs remaining on the target. Then play another round. Keep going until one player wins. You can play ice shuffleboard individually or in teams.

Snow Snake

Popular among several North American Indian groups, snow snake involves hurling a long stick along an icy track. Just as in javelin-throwing, the idea is to see whose stick can travel the farthest.

Snow snake is played on an empty snow-covered lot or field. It can be played on a hillside or on the flat ground. Different groups have devised their own rules and you may want to make your own version to fit the space available to you.

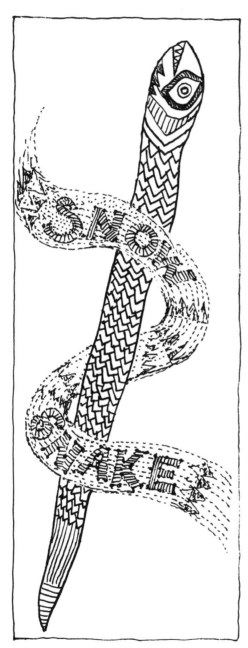

The traditional snake is a straight piece of hickory or maple five feet to ten feet long, one inch or more in diameter. One end is tapered to resemble a tail and the other is carved to look like the snake's head. The Indians oiled and seasoned the wood for several months before carving and finally waxing it. They often added lead weights to the head to make the snake travel faster. A finger groove was carved at the throwing end. Experts had a whole collection of snow snakes in different shapes and weights, each designed for specific weather conditions: powder snow, wet, windswept.

For a simpler snake, find a straight branch three feet to four feet long and about two inches thick. Peel off the bark and whittle a head on one end, a tapered tail on the other. You might want to personalize your snake by adding decorative carving or painting on eyes or other markings.

One way to play the game is to make a hard-packed track

by dragging a log about eight inches to twelve inches in diameter through the snow. If there are only a few inches of snow, pack down an even stretch, making a shallow groove for the snake to travel in. If there is deep snow, you can form a trough and then build up the banks a couple of feet high on each side. If the weather is cold, sprinkle track and sides with water to make a frozen (very fast) track. Your track can be straight or it can curve, conforming to the contours of the land.

To play the game, hold your index finger against the tail end and then steady the snake with your thumb and other fingers. Run to the starting line and throw the snake with an underhand motion. The object is to see whose snake goes the farthest in a given number of tries. You can compete individually or you can form teams. Decide how many points make a game. Score one point for the longest throw in each round. If you are playing in teams, add an extra point if the two longest throws in a round are made by two players on the same team.

The Cree Indians in Canada favor a shorter, thicker snow snake as well as a shorter track. The track (sixty feet or longer) is formed along a hillside by sliding a log. The track is then sprayed with water and allowed to ice over to make it slick. Snow barriers are constructed across it at various intervals. The object is to get the snake to pass through the barriers without jumping out of the track.

International matches are held between Canadian and U.S. snow-snake teams. In serious competition, on an iced track, snow snakes travel over 120 m.p.h. and cover a distance of over three-quarters of a mile.

4
WINTER EATING

Preserving Food

We all know that food must be stored in a cold place if it is to stay fresh. Many rural parts of our country were without electricity until the middle of this century, but that didn't keep people from preserving food. The icehouse, a common and important outbuilding on many farms, was a windowless structure built on a stone foundation strong enough to support lots of weight. It usually had double walls (some had triple or quadruple thicknesses) with a space of about half a foot between them. The space was filled with sawdust, hay, or leaves to provide lots of insulation. When you wear a down-filled jacket, the idea is to contain the heat generated by your body and to keep the cold air out. In this case, the purpose of the insulation was to keep the cold in and the warmer air *out*. Sometimes icehouses were built into a hillside, nearly underground, with just one side facing out, to take advantage of the earth's natural insulation. Farmers often built a cool chamber below the main floor, where they could store their fruits and dairy products, taking advantage of the cooling properties of the ice above.

Commercial ice harvesting was an important seasonal industry

61

in America from the 1840s up until about seventy years ago. The ice harvesters plowed the frozen ponds and lakes with horse- or mule-drawn scrapers. They then hitched a team to a sharp steel plow and worked back and forth, scoring the ice in a grid pattern that made it look like a checkerboard. Working by hand, they used sharp saws and chisels to cut free heavy blocks of ice. The blocks were then stored in the icehouse in anticipation of the summer demand. Some farmers cut their own ice, while others bought ice blocks from a commercial outfit.

Ice harvesting took place mostly in the North, where the rivers and lakes accumulated several feet of ice. Commercial icehouses also sprung up in the southern and western states, either alongside a navigable river or near a railroad since boats and trains were the two means of shipping ice to warmer parts of the country.

Before the invention of iceboxes, farmers stored their perishables in springhouses. As the name implies, these were built directly over or right next to a spring outlet, simple buildings made from stone or brick, including the floor. Crocks of milk and butter were stored in the channels that were built into the floor. Cool water from deep beneath the earth flowed through the channels, keeping the crocks at about 50°F. even on a hot midsummer day.

The most reliable way to preserve meat was by smoking it, and the smokehouse was another common farm fixture, particularly in parts of the country where hunting was the major source of table meat. Because thieves often tried to make off with a well-smoked ham, smokehouses were usually built close to the main farmhouse. Basically a draft-free smoke chamber, the smokehouse might be built from boards, tightly caulked and nailed together, or from mortared stone or bricks. It had a dirt floor, usually containing a fire pit several feet deep, which was filled with stones or mortar.

When the smokehouse was in use, a small smoldering fire was kindled in the pit. The fire eventually consumed nearly all the oxygen

in the smokehouse, leaving behind a thick cloud of smoke. Meat was hung on racks to smoke, a process that took days. The taste of the finished smoked product depended on the type of fuel used to feed the fire. Hickory, corncobs, and fruitwoods were favored.

Another way the farmer preserved food for the winter months was by storing it in his root cellar, an underground storage space dug into a hillside near the farmhouse or directly under the farmhouse floor. This was the perfect place to keep foods that needed to be kept cool yet frost free—root crops like carrots, potatoes, and turnips. The vegetables were stored in alternating layers with sand, sawdust, or hay. The modern-day basement grew out of the practice of digging a root cellar right beneath the farmhouse floor.

Still another way of preserving food is to dry it. "Schnitz" is a Pennsylvania Dutch word referring to any type of dried apples. In Colonial days, apples were cored and cut into rings. The rings were hung on strings from the rafters or near the fireplace. Sometimes they were placed in cooling ovens. To make your own schnitz, you'll need apples, wax paper, and cookie sheets. Core the unpeeled apples and cut into half-inch thick rings. Cover cookie sheets with wax paper; arrange apple slices in single layers. Preheat oven to 150°

and bake slices for several hours, until moisture evaporates and they are firm to the touch. For a traditional Early American snack, mix dried apple rings with raisins. Place schnitz in a tightly closed paper bag and store in a cool, dry place. It will last indefinitely.

Early American Apple Riddle: How many seeds are there in an apple? How many apples are there in a seed?

Another way of preserving fruit is to make peach leather or peach paper, a winter sweet much favored in Colonial times. You'll need two pounds of dried apricots, one pound of dried peaches, powdered

sugar, wax paper, a rolling pin, and a breadboard or other flat work surface. Finely chop the apricots and the peaches, and mix together. Dust board or work surface and rolling pin with powdered sugar. Take a small ball of fruit mixture and roll out to ⅛ inch thick. Cut into strips. Roll strips lengthwise into tight rolls and wrap individually in wax paper. Repeat process until you've used up all the fruit. Peach leather makes a delicious high-energy snack.

Indian Pudding

The early settlers were introduced to maize, or corn, a native grain, by the Indians. Accustomed to oatmeal and porridge, they soon developed a similar way of serving corn—cornmeal mush, otherwise known as Indian pudding. Sometimes it goes under the name of hasty pudding. Today this hearty dish is usually served as a dessert. Here's how to make your own:

1 cup cornmeal	½ teaspoon salt
1 cup cold water	1 tablespoon sugar
3 cups boiling water	Ice cream or whipped cream (optional)

Combine cornmeal and cold water; set aside. Bring 3 cups of water to a boil in a heavy saucepan. Add the salt. Add the cornmeal and water mixture, stirring steadily to make sure it doesn't get lumpy. Bring to a boil and then lower heat. Continue to cook over low heat, stirring occasionally, for about ten minutes or until very thick. Serve warm, sprinkled with sugar, or try it with ice cream or whipped cream. Makes three to four servings.

Jerky

Trappers, settlers, explorers, and Indian hunters all satisfied their hunger on jerky during the cold winter months when fresh food

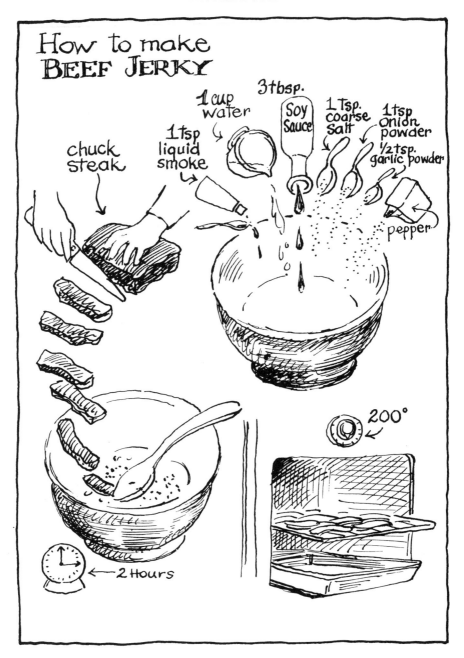

was hard to come by and on long trips anytime of the year. Jerky is dried meat (and sometimes fish), and it gets its name from the fact that it had to be pulled and jerked from the teeth as it was chewed. It was commonly prepared by soaking meat in brine (a combination of salt and water) and then drying it over a small fire. It was usually made from deer, buffalo, elk, caribou, moose, or beef. Jerky was eaten "as is," turned into stews, or pounded into tiny pieces called pemmican. Berries, wild greens, and herbs were added for flavor. To make mincemeat, apples, suet, and spices were added.

To make your own jerky, you'll need one pound of lean chuck steak, partly frozen so that it's easy to cut into thin strips. You'll also need one cup of water, one teaspoon of coarse salt, one teaspoon of liquid smoke (check your supermarket), three tablespoons soy sauce, one teaspoon onion powder, ½ teaspoon garlic powder, and a dash of black pepper.

Cut all the fat away from the meat and slice meat into strips, cutting along the grain. Mix all the other ingredients together in a large bowl. Add the strips and let them sit for at least two hours.

Preheat oven to 200°F. Place strips on a rack over a broiler pan. Leave door slightly open. Strips are done when they are hard and dry, which will take twenty to thirty hours.

How to Tap a Sugar Maple and Make Your Own Syrup

Check the label on the maple-syrup bottle on your kitchen shelf. If it contains three percent maple syrup consider yourself lucky. Some brands contain only one or two percent and others have none at all. Most commercial syrups are based on a combination of sugar syrup, corn syrup, and artificial flavorings.

One hundred percent pure maple syrup is the rich sweet liquid found mostly in country stores and specialty food shops. It is delicious and it is expensive. This is the sugar that sustained our forefathers when they could not afford the refined sweeteners from far off parts of the world. According to Indian legend, the old Earth Mother Nokomis was responsible for the production of the first maple syrup. She simply bored a hole in a sugar maple tree and the liquid that flowed forth was pure syrup. Her grandson, Manabush, thought this process was too easy. Lest the Indians become lazy, Manabush decided to make them work for their sweetener. He climbed to the top of a sugar maple and showered it with water, thus turning the water to sap. And ever since, making syrup has not been an easy task.

The fact of the matter is that syrup is about ninety-seven percent water and three percent maple-sugar content. In order to make a single gallon of maple syrup, you must boil down thirty-five gallons of sap. Taking the math a step further, you will need almost four and a half gallons of sap to produce a single pint of pure maple syrup. Now you should begin to understand why pure maple syrup is so expensive.

The New England Indians used to boil down their sap by pouring it into hollow logs and chucking in heated stones. In the nineteenth century, white men took to the woods on snowshoes, leading horse-drawn sledges with enough gear and provisions to last a week or more while they set about gathering sap. Today most sap is reduced to the syrup stage, but in Colonial times it was often boiled down even further to form blocks of maple sugar. These blocks were stored

in cool cellars and the Colonists chipped away at them whenever they needed a sweetener.

Although trucks, tractors, and skimobiles have replaced the horse-drawn sledge, modern maple-syrup manufacturers remain at the mercy of the elements. The flow of sap in the sugar maple is still Mother Nature's province. Until she blesses us with the right combination of warm days and cold, subfreezing nights, the collection of sap cannot begin. Most syrup makers agree that the sap runs best when the days are mild and the nighttime temperatures dip just below the freezing mark.

The sugar maple itself is a work of genius. In the summertime, the cells of the maple leaf synthesize a simple sugar. This sugar is converted into starch and stored in the roots and trunk of the tree. When autumn arrives and the maple leaves turn brilliant red, yellow, and orange, the tree becomes inactive. It keeps to itself all winter, but come spring the chemistry is back at work again. By the time the sap begins to flow, the original sugar (glucose) has been converted to a more complicated sugar (sucrose).

If you have several maple trees in your yard or if your neighbors will give you permission to use their trees, you can tap them yourself. To be sure that the trees are old enough so that you can tap them without doing any damage, measure the diameter of each trunk about two feet up from the ground. Do not tap any trees that measure less than twelve inches across.

Using a brace and ⅜-inch bit, bore a hole one to two inches into the tree trunk, four feet or less from the ground. Try to bore the hole directly above a vigorous root or directly below a strong branch. You will need to make one hole for the first twelve inches the tree measures and another for each additional six inches. If the tree measures twenty-four inches, you will need to make three holes.

After the holes have been drilled, drive a metal spout, or spile, into each one. These can be purchased very inexpensively at a large

hardware store or an agricultural supply outlet. Each spile has a hook on it that should be positioned downward so that a bucket can be hung from it. You can buy covered sap buckets or use clean household buckets after straining the sap through cheesecloth to remove any leaves, bits of bark, or other debris that may have fallen in. Because sap ferments quickly, it is wise to collect it each day, storing it in the refrigerator until you are ready to make syrup.

As noted earlier, you need four and a half gallons of sap to make a single pint of syrup. Small batches like this can be boiled down on the kitchen stove but the sugaring off (as this process is called) can take all day and must be watched carefully. Water is removed from the sap by steaming it at 170°F., never permitting it to come to a boil. You will need a candy thermometer.

It is important to have an adult supervise this process because it involves a large amount of very hot liquid. It is also important that the sugaring off take place in a well-ventilated room. Otherwise a sticky film of condensation, particularly harmful to wallpaper, will soon coat the walls.

A second method of reducing the sap involves boiling the liquid for a much shorter period of time. This process may take only an hour or two or it may take considerably longer, depending upon the sugar content of the sap. This is a very delicate process and one that must be handled by an adult. Sap is extremely flammable and boils over easily, so it must be watched every second. Be certain to use a candy thermometer. The syrup is ready when it reaches 219°F. Store the syrup in a clean, covered glass container in the refrigerator.

The next time you have a fresh snowfall, snack on "sugar-on-snow," a treat prepared by our ancestors in celebration of a successful sugaring season. Heat maple syrup to 250°–252°F. Without stirring, pour the hot syrup immediately onto a bowl of clean snow. It will form a glassy sheet of candy bearing a strong resemblance to taffy. If you cannot tap your own maple trees, you can make sugar-on-snow from purchased pure maple syrup. You cannot make it using one of the commercial brands containing only a small percentage of maple syrup.

Pulling Taffy

If you like to cook with friends, you ought to try a taffy pull. This was a popular activity a hundred years ago. Basically, you have a chance to get sticky and silly together while making delicious candy.

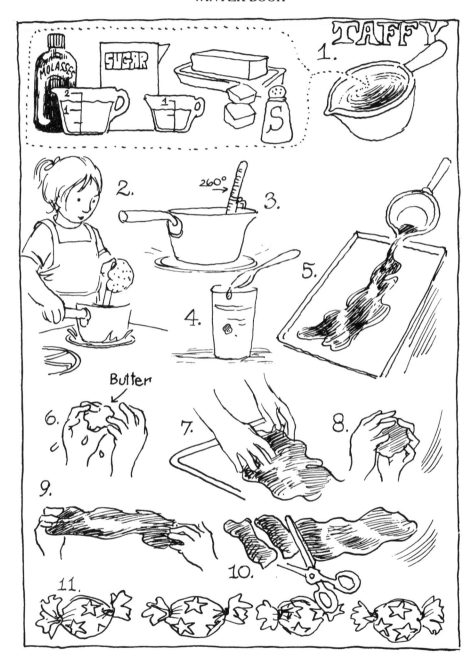

Making taffy can be very messy and a bit tricky, and it also requires handling very hot syrup, so it's best to have an adult help out. Be sure you have a candy thermometer on hand before starting. Here are two recipes to try:

Molasses Taffy	Peppermint Taffy
1 ½ cups light molasses	1 ½ cups sugar
¾ cup sugar	½ cup light syrup
2 tablespoons butter	¼ cup water
dash of salt	2 tablespoons butter
	salt
	½ teaspoon peppermint extract

Combine all ingredients in a heavy saucepan. Stir occasionally. Cook to hard-ball stage, 260°F. on a candy thermometer. Drop a bit of mixture in cold water; if it forms a hard ball, it's ready. Now pour the taffy on a buttered platter. As it cools, fold edges toward center. When it is cool enough to handle, you're ready to pull taffy.

(Note: If you are making the peppermint recipe, this is the time to divide the taffy in half. Add red food coloring to one chunk, kneading it in until the taffy gets pink.)

Before starting to pull, butter your hands generously. Pull a handful of taffy off the platter. Knead it in your hands, and then pull and stretch it. Pull it into long strips, and then cut strips into individual pieces with scissors. Wrap each piece in wax paper, twisting the ends. If you are making peppermint taffy, pull the white, then pull the pink, and then twist the two strands together.

5
CELEBRATIONS

Hanukkah

Hanukkah, which is celebrated for eight days beginning on the twenty-fifth day of the lunar month of Kislev (which falls in November or December) is a joyous midwinter festival that commemorates the victory of the Jews of Palestine, led by Judas Maccabeus, over the Syrians in 165 B.C. When the Maccabees returned to their temple after the war, they found only enough sacred oil to burn for one day. Miraculously, that tiny supply continued to burn for eight days. Light, then, is an important symbol in this midwinter celebration. The word Hanukkah in Hebrew means dedication, and Hanukkah is known both as the Feast of Dedication and the Festival of Lights.

The importance of light in this celebration dovetails with early folk customs in which ceremonial fires were lit at winter solstice to urge the sun back into a pattern of long days and short nights. Hanukkah, therefore, can be seen as having seasonal as well as historical roots.

During Hanukkah, candles are lit each evening symbolizing the eight days the oil burned in the temple. The Hanukkah menorah is a candelabra with places for nine candles—one for each night of

the celebration and one to hold the Shammash or "servant candle," which is used to light the others. Blessings are said over the Shammash before it is used. After the appropriate number of candles has been lit for that evening and the Shammash has been returned to its place, there is another chant. After that, children usually receive a gift.

Latkes

Potato pancakes or "latkes" are a traditional Hanukkah food, as are other foods cooked in oil, since oil is so important in the Hanukkah story. They are fun to make and delicious to eat.

4 large potatoes
1 small onion
1 egg
1 teaspoon baking powder
1 tablespoon matzo meal

½ teaspoon salt
½ teaspoon pepper
2 tablespoons flour
oil for frying

Peel and coarsely grate potatoes and onion. Drain well. Add egg and remaining ingredients. Drop from spoon into hot oil, about ¼ inch deep. Fry until brown on both sides. Serve hot. Great with apple sauce.

All About the Dreidel

The dreidel is a four-sided spinning top good for playing games of chance. At a time when Jews were forbidden to practice their religion in certain places, they used to play dreidel games to hide the fact that they were praying together. You can make your own simple dreidel by following these directions:

Begin by using a ruler to mark off a three-inch square of heavy cardboard. Cut out the square. At the center of each edge of the square, using paints or markers, draw one of the four Hebrew characters shown below:

NUN = nisht = nothing
GIMMEL = gantz = all
HEY = halb = half
SHIN = shtel = put in 1

The characters are actually initials for *Nes Gadol Hayah Sham,* which means "a great miracle happened there."

When the characters have dried, push a short pencil through the center of the square. Now you're ready to spin your dreidel.

Each person playing the traditional dreidel game is given the same number of pennies or gold-paper-covered chocolate coins. Each puts one coin in the center of the playing area (the "pot"). Each player then spins the dreidel in turn and follows the directions on the side that lands facing up. If GIMMEL is up, for example, the player takes all the coins from the middle. If SHIN is up, he puts in one, and if HEY is up, he gets half. For NUN, he does nothing. Whenever the pot is empty or has only one coin, each player must add two. The object is to win all the coins.

Here is the traditional dreidel song, which is fun to sing as you play the game.

MY DREIDEL

I had a little dreidel, I made it out of clay,
And when it's dry and ready, the dreidel I shall play.

O dreidel, dreidel, dreidel, I made it out of clay
O dreidel, dreidel, dreidel, now dreidel I shall play.

It has a lovely body with leg so short and thin,
And when it is all tired, it drops and then I win.

O dreidel, dreidel, dreidel with leg so short and thin,
O dreidel, dreidel, dreidel, it drops and then I win.

My dreidel's always playful, it loves to dance and spin,
A happy game of dreidel, come play, now let's begin.

O dreidel, dreidel, dreidel, it loves to dance and spin,
O driedel, dreidel, dreidel, come play, now let's begin.

Christmas

Winter celebrations began long before Hanukkah and Christmas. The Romans, Gauls, Teutons, and Britons worshipped the sun as a source of light and life. Their midwinter festival was called Saturnalia, honoring Saturn, their god of agriculture.

The centuries passed, and with them came the birth of Christ and the growth of Christianity. By A.D. 350, Emperor Constantine had established Christianity as the state religion of the Roman Empire. As Christianity spread across the globe, so too did the practice of celebrating Christmas as the day on which Christ was born. The observance often included a mix of pagan and religious customs. These customs developed around a set of symbols that continue to be important today.

The tradition of the Christmas tree has roots that extend back

to pagan times. Egyptians brought date palms into their homes to celebrate the winter solstice and the Romans decorated trees in honor of Saturnalia. The ancient Druids also decorated trees in honor of their gods, and wandering Jewish tribes used branches as decorations. The Christmas tree as we know it today originated in Germany. When the German Hessian soldiers came to America during the Revolutionary War, they brought the custom with them.

The custom of giving gifts long predates Christianity. The Magi (the Three Kings) gave the first Christmas gifts, but the Romans gave winter gifts during Saturnalia. By the sixteenth century, gift giving centered on children. They typically received three different types of presents: pleasing (chocolates), practical (writing implements), disciplinary (a birch rod for administering spankings).

The Druids and early Scandinavians originated the custom of burning a Yule log. Ancient tribesmen regarded fire as a symbol of home and safety. The Scandinavians believed that the sun was fastened to a big wheel that stops for twelve days during the winter solstice, so they lit a continually burning fire to see them through that period. The English adapted that custom, burning a Yule log on Christmas Eve. They thought it was good luck to sit on the log before burning it, bad luck if the fire went out too quickly. And they liked to save a piece of the log to kindle next year's Yule log.

Many people complain today that the observance of Christmas has become over-commercialized. One of the best ways to avoid this trend is to put your energy into homemade Christmas projects instead of spending all your time shopping. Here are some ideas to get you started:

Make Your Own Advent Calendar

To make your own Advent calendar, you'll need several colorful magazines that you can cut up. It doesn't matter what year they're from, but they should be November and December issues so that they have lots of Christmas pictures in them. If you have a collection of old Christmas cards, you can use these.

You'll also need two large sheets of construction paper, glue, star stickers, glitter, markers, pencil, a stapler, and scissors.

1. Begin by outlining a Christmas tree on one piece of construction paper. Cut out the tree.

2. Then draw twenty-four small squares on the tree, varying from about one inch × one inch to two inches × two inches. Use a ruler to make the lines straight. Distribute the squares all over the tree, thinking of them as decorations.

3. Cut along three sides of each square. Fold door open on uncut hinge. When you have done all twenty-four, place the tree on top of the second piece of paper.

4. Trace the window openings on to the second sheet with a pencil, so that when you remove the tree you see twenty-four squares on the bottom sheet.

5. Cut out twenty-four Christmas pictures from your magazines or cards, one for each square. You can cut them a little larger than the squares; just be sure that the part you want showing fits in the square. Glue one picture to each square.

6. Staple the tree to the bottom sheet, matching the window openings to the squares.

7. Close each window with a star sticker.

8. Number the doors from one to twenty-four.

9. Decorate the tree with markers or glitter.

Now you're ready to hang up your Advent calendar and to use it to count down the days until Christmas. Beginning on December first, open one door each day, starting with the door marked No. 1. Of course, you already know what the pictures are because you made the calendar. You and a friend could make one for each other so that you could be surprised. Advent calendars also make good early presents for sisters and brothers and even for grown-ups.

Build a Gingerbread House

Making the Gingerbread. Sift or mix together:

   4 cups flour
   2 tablespoons sugar
   1 ½ teaspoons baking powder
   ½ teaspoon baking soda
   ½ teaspoon salt
   1 ½ teaspoons ginger

Melt together 1 cup molasses and ½ cup butter. When cool, mix in ¼ cup milk and all the dry ingredients from above. Form dough into two balls, wrap in wax paper and chill.

Making the Frosting. To make the "glue" that holds the house together, beat two egg whites together with ¼ teaspoon cream of tartar. Beat in 1 cup confectioner's sugar and beat for ten minutes. Add 1 more cup confectioner's sugar and continue to beat for *ten more minutes.* That's a lot of beating, but it's what makes the glue stick.

Assembling the House. Cut out four pieces of cardboard that are seven inches wide and ten inches long. Two are for the side walls and two are for the roof of the house. Then cut out two pieces of cardboard, each seven inches × eleven inches, for the gabled ends of the house. Make a line across each end wall, dividing it into four-inch and

85

seven-inch sections. Then make a mark at the top center of the four-inch section. Make two cuts down from this mark to the line, to form the pointed gable.

If you want to have windows or doors in your house, cut openings out of the cardboard pieces where you want them.

Line cookie sheets with wax paper. Roll out dough on floured surface. Using cardboard pieces as patterns, cut out two side walls, two end walls, and two roof pieces. Cut the pieces a bit larger than the pattern. Cut windows and doors.

Preheat oven to 350° and bake the gingerbread for twelve to fifteen minutes. (If you want stained glass windows in your house, crush some colored hard candies, remove the gingerbread from the oven after ten minutes, fill window spaces with crushed candy, and return to oven for several more minutes.) While the gingerbread is baking, use masking tape to assemble cardboard pieces into a house. Tape house to a cardboard base.

Let gingerbread cool completely. Then use frosting to glue the pieces onto the cardboard model. When your house is assembled and the glue has dried, use more frosting to glue on candy decorations. Maybe you'll use extra frosting to create a snowy yard. You might want to fill it with friendly creatures; use animal crackers. Let your imagination really take over and you'll find yourself with a gingerbread house that is absolutely the only one of its kind.

Pinecone and Nut Wreath

Decorate your front door or a wall with a large wreath. You'll need an assortment of pinecones, nuts, acorns, and seedpods, as well as a piece of corrugated cardboard, ribbon, white glue, and plastic spray varnish. Before beginning your wreath, place pinecones on a cookie sheet covered with wax paper; bake in 300° oven for ten minutes to bleed out pitch.

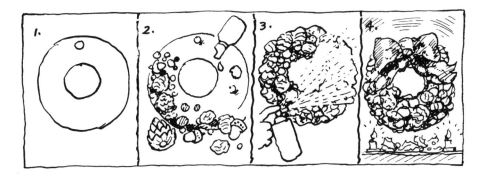

1. Cut the cardboard into a ring the size you want your finished wreath to be.

2. Punch a hole at the top of the cardboard so you can thread a piece of ribbon through for hanging. If your wreath is going to be large and heavy, you might want to make two holes and thread the ribbon through both to distribute the weight.

3. Use white glue to fasten pinecones, nuts, acorns, and seedpods into place, completely covering the cardboard ring. Let the glue dry thoroughly.

4. Spray the whole wreath with plastic varnish.

5. When completely dry, add ribbon. Your wreath is ready for hanging.

6. You might want to experiment by making small wreaths. Follow directions above, but when you have finished gluing materials on one side, let dry and then turn over and do the other side. Spray each side. Small wreaths can be used as tree decorations or they can be hung in doorways or wherever else you choose. Your wreaths are reusable. Be sure to pack them away carefully when the holidays are over so you can enjoy them again next year.

Other Ideas for Christmas Ornaments from Natural Materials

1. Dip pinecones in self-polishing wax. While still wet, spray

with hair spray and sprinkle with glitter. Tie on ribbon for hanging.

2. Paint walnuts gold or silver. To hang, use white glue to attach gold cord loop.

3. Using a needle and strong thread, make popcorn and cranberry chains. For best results, use ripe cranberries and stale popcorn. Instead of trying to make very long chains, make three-foot lengths and then tie them together (helps avoid tangling).

Your New Year's Celebration

Ask your parents if they will help you plan a special slumber party, one that lasts from this year until next. If you have brothers or sisters, include them and their friends in your plans, too, for a party that will make this an evening to remember.

New Year's Eve is a time both to renew your sense of the past and to look forward to the future. Ask each guest to bring along an old home movie or a collection of snapshots from the time he or she was a baby. Have a screening and allow each "star" to narrate his own film (or set of photos). Of course, you will want to make your own contribution to the screening as well.

Ask each guest to bring along a baby picture and ask your parents to assign a number to each picture. Supply paper and pencils and see who can identify the most baby pictures.

Another good New Year's Eve game is trivia, an exercise in recalling the past. Ask your parents to prepare questions dealing with famous moments in sports, world events, school and community events, and the arts and entertainment world. Or, have each guest contribute several questions. You might ask questions like these: Who won the World Series this year? Who got married in a prime-time TV situation comedy? How many baseball cards came in a pack this year? Which classroom won field day?

Because New Year's Eve is a sentimental time, avoid cut-throat competition by rewarding all correct answers instead of adding up the total points and choosing one winner. A shiny gold-paper-covered chocolate coin could be awarded for each correct answer. You might explain that in Spain, hundreds of years ago, it was believed that a person fortunate enough to have a gold coin in his or her pocket on New Year's Day would never want for cash in the year ahead.

If you have a fireplace in your home, you can go even further to assure good luck in the coming year. Explain to your guests that chestnuts are traditional lucky charms. Roast them in the ashes, with help from adults (you need to cut an X in the back of each one with a sharp knife to keep them from exploding in the fire). You can also talk about other foods traditionally associated with good luck. Some American Indian tribes ate acorns and salmon on New Year's Day to symbolize abundant food supplies in the year ahead. In Texas and other parts of the Southwest, it is considered good luck to eat black-eyed peas on January 1st. On the other hand, some cultures felt it necessary to refrain from certain foods to insure good luck. The ancient Chinese would not eat rice on New Year's Day and the Germans avoided dumplings.

One tasty custom that is fun to adopt is that of the Albanian lucky cake. Bake a cake and mix a gold-paper-covered chocolate coin or a real coin wrapped in a piece of foil in the batter. Whoever finds it is destined to have a fabulous New Year. You might even decide to bake other small surprises into the cake, each one wrapped in foil, so that each guest finds a treasure.

In addition to games and food, a New Year's Eve party requires noisemakers. Collect coffee cans, dried beans, uncooked rice, small pebbles, yarn and fabric scraps, and odd bits like feathers and shiny paper in the weeks preceding the party. Take out your white glue, construction paper, and magic markers, and have each guest make his or her own noisemaker. After decorating the coffee cans and filling them with a handful of pebbles, beans, or rice, or a combination

of these, cap them with their plastic lids. Wooden spoons or plain old sticks make satisfactory drumsticks.

Primitive people used to make noise at New Year's to scare away evil spirits. In some parts of Russia, people used to beat the corners of their houses with sticks to scare away the evil spirits, and the Chinese set off firecrackers at their ancestors' graves for the same reason. In Switzerland and Germany, boys and girls marched around their towns beating drums early New Year's Day to banish harmful beings. Again, the idea was to get rid of any of last year's nasty demons who might be lurking about hoping to spoil the fresh new year. Use your noisemakers to herald in the midnight hour, before settling down in your sleeping bags. Happy New Year!

How to Say "Happy New Year" Seven Ways

Chinese	Guo nien!
German	Gluckliches neues Jahr!
French	Bonne Annee!
Italian	Buon Anno!
Norwegian	Godt nyt år!
Russian	Snovom godom!
Spanish	Feliz año neuvo!

Martin Luther King Day

A black civil rights leader and clergyman, Martin Luther King devoted much of his life to overcoming racial discrimination. He was born in Georgia in 1929 and became minister of the Dexter Avenue Baptist Church in Montgomery, Alabama. During the 1950s and '60s, a time when black children in some parts of our country were sent to separate (and often poorer quality) schools from white children, Dr. King worked hard to change unfair laws.

At that time it was not unusual to see public rest rooms and drinking fountains in the South with signs that said White Only, meaning that black people couldn't use them. Black people were told where to sit on public buses (in the back) and some restaurants refused to serve them. All of these injustices are forms of racial discrimination.

Dr. King was committed to nonviolence. He believed that instead of fighting, black people should work for equal rights by electing public officials who would change the unfair laws. In many places, however, blacks were prevented or discouraged from registering to vote. He also encouraged black people to work for change by refusing to patronize businesses that discriminated against them.

Throughout his life, Dr. King led boycotts, marches, and sit-ins around the country, working to change unfair laws without violence. He was the target of vicious name-calling, he was beaten, and he was jailed seventeen times. Yet he continued to preach nonviolence and to work toward change.

One of Dr. King's finest moments occurred in the summer of 1963 when he led a huge peace march in Washington, D.C. Thousands of people, black and white, came from all over the country to show their support of his efforts to secure equal rights. He delivered his famous "I have a dream" speech, in which he spoke eloquently of his hopes for the future. In 1964, Dr. King's efforts received

International recognition when he was given the Nobel Peace Prize, awarded annually to the individual who has done the most to bring peace to the world.

The thousands of people who gathered in Washington, D.C., and in other cities across the country, united in their desire for racial justice, often joined together to express their feelings in song. One of the most popular protest songs of the day was "We Shall Overcome," which begins like this:

> We shall overcome
> We shall overcome
> Black and white together,
> We shall overcome some day.
> Oh deep in my heart, I do believe
> We shall overcome some day.

Dr. King's life came to an abrupt end when he was killed by an assassin in 1968. Today his birthday, January 15th (or a day close to it), is observed as a federal holiday.

Groundhog Day

Groundhog Day is an offshoot of Candlemas Day, February 2nd, a religious observance that features the blessing of candles. The British regarded Candlemas as the end of the holiday season and believed that leaving Christmas decorations up beyond this date was unlucky. English and German settlers brought the tradition to the U.S.

Europeans also believed that on this date bears and badgers emerged from their burrows. If they saw their shadows, the animals would be frightened and would retreat back into their winter lodgings, signifying another stretch of cold, wintry weather.

In the U.S., the superstition applies primarily to groundhogs, although badgers and hedgehogs are taken into account in some parts of the country. If the groundhog emerges into the sunshine and sees his shadow, he is supposedly frightened back into his hole for another six weeks of hibernation. For the farmer, this means that there will be six more weeks of cold weather and that he can expect a poor crop next year. But if the weather is cloudy and the groundhog remains above ground (having failed to see his shadow), an early spring is predicted. This is one of the few superstitions in which sunshine is interpreted as a bad omen. Pennsylvania, which has heavily German roots, is a stronghold of groundhog clubs and fables and celebrations concerning the superstition.

Because it beckons in the

coldest weather we experience, Groundhog Day has become a popular weather-forecasting date. Another Candlemas superstition offers sound advice to the anxious farmer:

> Half the wood and half the hay,
> You should have on Candlemas Day.

This makes a lot of sense. With half the cold weather season behind and half still ahead, the prudent farmer will probably still have half his stores remaining to see him through.

Valentine's Day

Who Was St. Valentine?
St. Valentine was actually Valentinus, a Christian priest in third-century Rome who was condemned to death because he refused to worship Roman gods. As legend goes, while in jail awaiting execution Valentinus became friends with the jailer's blind daughter, whose eyesight was restored through his prayers. On the eve of his death, he wrote her a farewell message, which he signed, "From your Valentine." Valentinus died on February 14, the date we observe as Valentine's Day. In time, St. Valentine became known as the patron saint of lovers.

The origin of St. Valentine's Day has become lost in history but the most common explanation is that it grew out of the ancient Roman festival of Lupercalia, celebrated on February 15. On this day young people drew names from a clay urn to determine the identity of their true loves. Couples matched this way were expected to be in love at least until the next Lupercalia arrived. In the year A.D. 496, Pope Galasius changed Lupercalia from February 15 to St. Valentine's Day, February 14th. By the Middle Ages, the holiday was firmly established in England and Scotland.

Many customs have grown up around St. Valentine's Day. In ancient times, a young person would wrap names written on paper in pieces of clay, dropping the pieces in water. All of them would sink except the one bearing the name of one's true love, which would rise to the surface. Another tradition holds that the first young man a maiden sees on St. Valentine's Day will become her true love.

The Lupercalia ceremony of the young man choosing his beloved's name by lot took on a different form as the centuries passed. To take the element of chance out of the choice, a young man would write his name on a piece of paper and present it to the young lady of his choice on Valentine's Day. Eventually, young men began adding poetry to these love billets or notes.

There is no common agreement on when and where the custom of sending Valentine cards got started, but we do know that originally such cards were sent only by men. They were handmade at first. Some were pen-and-ink drawings, others were watercolors, and still others included silhouettes or cutouts.

Some men had difficulty writing poetry. They were probably relieved in the early 1820s when clever publishers came out with books like *The Polite Valentine Writer*, which provided verses for use in handmade cards. For example: "You are the girl I take delight in, much more than haddock, smelt, or whiting." Mass-produced Valentine cards first came on the scene in the mid-nineteenth century.

Because tomatoes were called love apples, many cards were made in the shape of tomatoes.

In this country, valentines appeared in the mid-1700s and were sent only by men. During the Civil War, however, women too began to send cards to their sweethearts. Many of these cards involved the use of clever puzzles like rebuses (combining pictures, letters, and words to form a message), cryptograms (codes), and acrostics (spelling from top to bottom, the first letter of each line forms a name or message).

There are lots of ways to make your own Valentine cards. Below you'll find a few examples. Use them as guidelines, adding your own imaginative touches. Try writing your own poetry or puzzle for the inside. If you want to send an anonymous card, you might like to include this verse, which comes from a 1927 edition of *The Delineator,* an early woman's magazine:

> To a friend:
> We scrap and fight
> But just the same,
> I love you best—
> Now guess my name!

Love Glove

A paper cutout in the shape of a hand was another popular love token a hundred years ago, when a man used to propose by asking for a woman's hand in marriage. Real gloves also became a popular Valentine gift. To make your own card in this tradition, fold a piece of construction paper in half and trace your own hand, with your wrist at the fold. Cut out the hand, leaving the fold as the card hinge. Inside, you can print this verse from a nineteenth century love glove:

CELEBRATIONS

> If that from Glove
> You take the G
> Then glove is love,
> Which I send thee.

Woven Inset Card

To make woven inset valentines, you'll need construction paper, tape, glue and bright wrapping paper, ribbon or fabric scraps. You'll also need scissors and a ruler.

Begin by folding a piece of construction paper in half to make the card itself. Take another piece of construction paper, fold in half the same way, and cut into two pieces along fold. Take one of the two pieces, fold in half lengthwise, and cut out the shape of half a heart. Unfold and lay flat. You'll have a piece the same size as the front of your card but with a heart-shaped hole in the center.

Now make the inset. Take the remaining, uncut piece of construction paper, which is also the same size as the front of the card. Trim half an inch from each side. Fold in half. Then use a ruler to draw lines across the paper from the fold to half an inch from the opposite side. Cut along the lines starting at the fold and continuing to the end of the line, half an inch from the edge of the paper. Be careful not to cut through to the opposite side. Open up and lay flat.

Begin weaving strips of scraps, over and under the rows of paper, all the way across. Alternate rows, so that if the first strip goes over the first bar of paper, the second one begins by going under that same bar. When you have finished weaving strips across, trim the edges of your inset and secure them with tape so that they don't come loose.

Now it's time to assemble your valentine. Place the piece with the cutout heart over the inset and glue it into place so that the

WOVEN INSET CARD

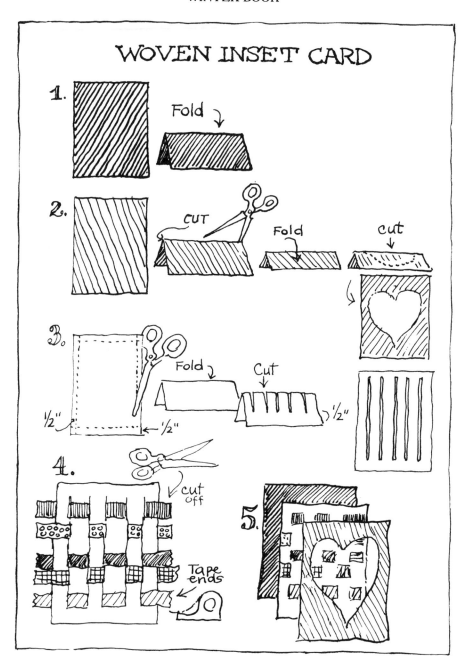

heart is filled with the inset. Then glue the whole inset piece to the front of the card. Write a Valentine message inside.

Carnation Sale

February can be a dreary month. With the excitement of the holidays far behind and a substantial chunk of cold weather still ahead, this is the ideal time to stir up some excitement. Try holding a Valentine's Day Carnation Sale. You can have fun and earn money for a worthwhile cause at the same time. Here's how it works.

Members of your group (scout troop, classmates, etc.) take advance orders for carnations to be delivered on Valentine's Day. When a customer orders a flower, he or she also gives you the name and address of the person to receive the carnation. You record this information in a small notebook and collect payment (charge twice the price you will have to pay for the flowers). Explain to your customer that on Valentine's Day you will deliver the carnation. If the recipient wants to find out the donor's name, however, he or she will have to pay fifty cents.

In planning your sale, consult first with a reliable florist. Ask if you can get a discount when you order a large number of flowers. Agree on a final deadline, the date on which you will file your order so the florist can guarantee you the right number of flowers on the big day. If you want to get fancy, you can offer flowers in different colors—pink for "I like you," red for "I love you"—making certain that you let the florist know exactly how many of each color you'll need.

This is a pleasant fund raiser to organize. Because purchasers pay in advance, you will have the cash to pay the florist for the flowers. Charging recipients to discover the name of their admirer adds fun and fattens your treasury at the same time. A Valentine's Day Carnation Sale offers a welcome change from the usual bake sales, raffles, and bazaars.

Presidents' Day

Abraham Lincoln and George Washington are the only two presidents whose birthdays are honored with a national holiday. Presidents' Day is celebrated the third Monday in February.

Abraham Lincoln's Birthday

Born on February 12, 1809, in a log cabin in Kentucky, Abraham Lincoln became our country's sixteenth president. Due to his leadership, the country emerged united following the devastating War Between the States (the Civil War). Lincoln never lost touch with the common people. He was supposedly in the habit of advising his own children, "Don't drink, don't smoke, don't chew, don't swear, don't gamble, don't lie, don't cheat; love your fellowmen as well as God; love truth, love virtue, and be happy." His Emancipation Proclamation, issued on January 1, 1863, paved the way for the Thirteenth Amendment to the United States Constitution, which abolished slavery in all parts of the country.

Lincoln was assassinated by actor John Wilkes Booth while watching a play at Ford's Theatre in Washington, D.C., in April 1865. The funeral train carrying his body back to Illinois was greeted by thousands of weeping mourners as it made its way west.

In Albany, New York, workers at the New York Central yards say that Lincoln's funeral train still passes through each year on April 27. About midnight, the air seems to tense, a hush settles. Workers pause and wait. It is said that a phantom train with black drapes streaming in the wind and a coffin visible in the funeral car rushes by. When it is gone, the workers reset their watches because, they say, on the night Lincoln's funeral train passes through, the clocks are always found to be running slow in Albany.

To commemorate Lincoln's birth, you can make a simple log

cabin, following directions that appeared in a 1913 issue of *The Delineator,* a popular woman's magazine.

Materials:

brown construction paper strips, 2½ inches × 8 inches and 2½ inches × 6 inches
construction paper as desired for roof, doors, windows
white glue
shirt cardboard at least 9 inches × 7 inches, for cabin foundation
large pencil

Step-by-Step:

1. Roll the construction paper strips into cylinders, using the pencil as a foundation for rolling.

2. Glue two cylinders to the cardboard, crossed at the corners in log-cabin fashion, to make the foundation of the house.

3. Continue in this manner until house is desired height.

4. Fashion roof and other details as desired.

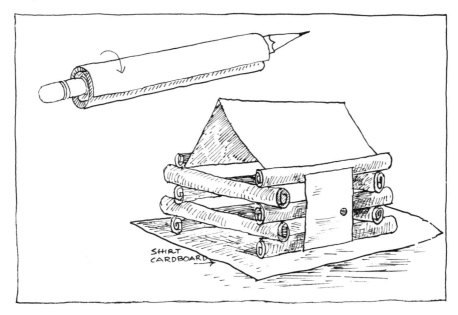

George Washington's Birthday

George Washington, known as the "Father of His Country," was our first president. He served as the commander in chief of the first American Army, which fought the Revolutionary War and won American independence from Great Britain. He also served as the president of the Constitutional Convention, which gathered in Philadelphia in 1787 to draw up the document that would govern the new nation.

There seems to be no truth in the story that when George Washington was about six years old, his father gave him his own hatchet. Having later chopped down one of his father's treasured cherry trees, and having been asked by his father who was responsible for the damage, George is said to have responded, "I cannot tell a lie, Father. I cut it down with my little hatchet." To create your own gumdrop-cherry-tree centerpiece in honor of George Washington's birthday, follow these instructions from a 1923 edition of *The Delineator.*

Materials:
 several short branches, spray painted brown or green
 floral wire
 green tissue paper or artificial leaves
 flowerpot of dirt
 circle of cardboard, painted green, to cover top of flowerpot
 red gumdrops, small
 needle and thread

Step-by-Step:
1. Wire several branches together to look like a tree and set securely in pot of dirt through a hole cut in the cardboard covering.
2. To make "cherries," thread pairs of gumdrops with flat ends facing about five inches apart. Knot and cut the thread at the small

end of each gumdrop, leaving them attached in pairs.

3. Twist two pairs and a spray of leaves together and hang over a branch. Place a tiny hatchet at the base of the tree if desired.

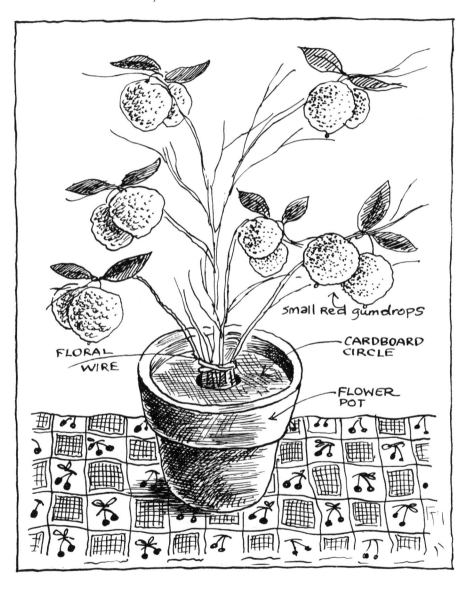

small Red gumdrops

CARDBOARD
CIRCLE

FLORAL
WIRE

FLOWER
POT

6
LAST THOUGHTS:
ASK ME
A RIDDLE

Ask Me a Riddle

In the 1880s, riddles provided popular and pleasant fireside entertainment on cold, blustery winter evenings. There are many types of riddles.

The true riddle describes one object in terms of another in order to confuse the listener. The first half is purposely misleading and the second half is accurate and straightforward. Here is a familiar example:

> Humpty Dumpty sat on a wall.
> Humpty Dumpty had a great fall.
> All the king's horses and all the king's men
> Couldn't put Humpty Dumpty together again.

What's Humpty Dumpty? An egg, of course. The riddler describes it as a person in order to befuddle the listener and then makes a "true" statement: he couldn't be put together again. Almost all so-called true riddles describe common objects or activities found around the home or farm.

Here are a few more to try out on your friends:

What has teeth but cannot eat?
(Answer: A comb or a saw.)

What runs all the way from Boston to New York and back again without moving? (Answer: The road.)

What has a head but can't think?
(Answer: A match or a pin.)

What has legs but cannot walk?
(Answer: A chair or a table.)

Four fingers and a thumb, yet flesh and bone have I none.
(Answer: A glove.)

And here's one in verse form:

> On the hill there is a house,
> In that house there is a closet,
> In that closet hangs a coat,
> In that coat is a pocket, and
> In that pocket is President Lincoln.
> (Answer: A penny.)

Best of all is the old English "Riddle Song," which has spread throughout America.

> I gave my love a cherry without any stone,
> I gave my love a chicken without any bone,
> I gave my love a ring without any end,
> I gave my love a baby and no crying.
>
> How can there be a cherry without any stone?
> How can there be a chicken without any bone?
> How can there be a ring without any end?
> How can there be a baby and no crying?

A cherry when it's blooming
  it has no stone,
A chicken in the egg
  it has no bone,
A ring when it's rolling
  it has no end,
A baby when it's sleeping
  there's no crying.

Puzzle and problem riddles were popular too. Here all the necessary information is provided; one just has to figure out how to make sense of it. Try these:

There is a mill with seven corners.
In each corner stand seven bags.
Upon each bag sit seven cats.
Each cat has seven kittens.
Then the miller and his wife come into the mill.
How many feet are now in the mill?
(Answer: Four. The cats have paws.)

How many feet are there on a lamb if you call a tail a foot? (Answer: Four. Calling a tail a foot doesn't make it one.)

Write down four 9's so that they will total one hundred. (Answer: 99 %.)

Two ducks in front of two ducks.
Two ducks behind two ducks.
Two ducks between two ducks.
How many ducks are there?
(Answer: Four.)

109

There were seven copy cats sitting on a fence.
One jumped off. How many were left?

(Answer: None.)

Conundrums involve a pun or play on words. Most of them appeared within the last century. Here are two to drive you crazy:

What is the difference between a ballerina and a duck?
(Answer: One goes quick on her beautiful legs, the other goes quack on her beautiful eggs.)

Can a leopard change his spots?
(Yes. When he is tired of one spot, he can go to another.)

Try inventing riddles of your own. You'll probably find them so much fun that you'll want to tell and solve them right into springtime!

Index

111